THE CAVE:

The True Story of Two Mysterious Deaths in an Underwater Labyrinth.

Dan Frolec

About *The Cave*

5.5 million people liked the animated video of the story on TikTok: "The Mystery While Diving"

619,000 people watched the YouTube video depicting the course of events: "Cave Exploring Gone WRONG | The Poganica Bay Cave Diving Disaster"

"I remember being so enamoured by this fantastic tale when Dan verbally told it to me a few years ago. Once I recovered from the amazing twists and turns of the story, I remember thinking 'this has to be a book', and now, here it is, for everyone to be taken on this breathless journey."
– **Kipper Eldridge**, Grammy and Emmy winning music producer.

"*The Cave* is a powerful and poignant, blow-by-blow account of this tragic event and its lasting impact. It's a must-read for all scuba diving enthusiasts."
– **Guy Creasey**, documentary editor who's been the recipient of Emmy and Bafta awards.

"What begins as an adventure among friends quickly turns into a dark descent into the abyss. But what makes Frolec's novel most disconcerting is that his nightmare is true. A haunting story of desperation, will, survival and determination."
– **Christopher Thompson**, co-founder of The Bridge Learning Center, former Director of Green School Bali and author of the novel *Butterfly: A Sibling's Story.*

"In a world full of managed stories, often not based on truth, Frolec's book stands out as being the real deal, totally authentic, so well written and with important messages about trust and survival."
– **Robert Swan, OBE**, the first person to walk to the North and South Poles and Founder of the 2041 Foundation.

"A captivating, true tale filled with unexpected twists that kept me hooked from beginning to end."
– **Ruben Stephenson**, Director of Kew Diving Services.

"Frolec's tale is a reminder of how anyone's life can suddenly take an unexpected and terrifying turn. Told with storytelling mastery, *The Cave* invites us to explore the depths of our own vulnerability and the darkness of those who might wrest us of agency."
– **Steve Stine**, author of *The Deep Earth Chronicles.*

"*The Cave* is a gripping, true-life adventure that masterfully blends camaraderie, suspense and the raw beauty of underwater exploration. Dan Frolec's vivid storytelling immerses readers in the world of passionate divers, capturing both the thrill of discovery and the haunting reality of loss. This book is a compelling tribute to friendship, trust and the unpredictable power of nature—a must-read for anyone drawn to real-life adventure and human resilience."
– **Alex Soldevila**, Creative Director and Board Member of Majestic Hotel Group.

"Frolec is clearly a man with a taste for adventure. For divers, this is an absolute must-read—a gripping, true tale of how tragedy can unfold in paradise. Not a survival story, this is a testament to friendship, resilience, and the bonds forged in the depths."
– **Stefano Azario**, imagemaker-at-large.

"This book is a nerve-wracking thriller based on a true story. The reader feels like they're right there, experiencing the drama that unfolded more than twenty years ago. Dan's matter-of-fact style will keep you engaged until the very end and, at the same time, wondering: 'How was it possible for them to survive and stay sane?'"
– **James Anders Banks**, author of *The Cowboy, the Empathy Kitten and the Cube.*

This book is based on a true story. It reflects the author's present recollections of experiences over time. Some names and characteristics have been changed, some events have been compressed, and some dialogues have been recreated.

First published 2026
by Rowanvale Books Ltd
The Gate
Keppoch Street
Roath
Cardiff
CF24 3JW
www.rowanvalebooks.com

A CIP catalogue record for this book is available from the British Library.
ISBN: 978-1-83584-125-9
eBook ISBN: 978-1-83584-126-6

Printed and bound in Great Britain by Bell & Bain Ltd, Glasgow

THE CAVE:

The True Story of Two Mysterious Deaths in an Underwater Labyrinth.

Dan Frolec

For Mirek, Oliver & Tomáš.

A story of death, survival, and trust.

Czech Republic, Prague, Podolí, July 2002

Now sitting in the pub, I must admit that this place is not our favourite locale, but it offers the closest reasonably priced beer to the pool. Simple wooden benches and tables, no tablecloths of course, obligatory paper coasters under the pints of beer to keep the tables dry. Not really possible, obviously, as the waiter behind the beer tap has to pour quickly to meet the unstoppable demand of a busy weekday night. At this time of the day the pub is full, mixing local regulars with the guys like us, most people drinking one pint after another.

We had gathered in the Podolka pub as usual to chat, unwind after the day at work, and chill out following our regular Tuesday swimming session. We are a bunch of good friends who dive together and must often rely on each other, both above- and underwater. We trust each other.

Marek, everyone calls him Pike, takes a sip of his beer, glancing around the table. He usually talks in a low voice. However, chatter in this busy place and clanking of the glasses force him to speak up. "So," he says, turning to Tom, "who is going to Croatia?"

Everyone looks at each other. *What?* can be seen on all our faces.

"I haven't had a chance to tell anyone yet!" Tom reacts quickly, with a somewhat apologetical face, skin on his head glistening.

"Well," says Pike with a gentle smile, "*Domani* is going to be available for one week in September. I can give you a special price, so let's go diving together."

Domani is an old but beautiful and functional sailing boat, which Pike sails around Croatia every summer, moving her to the Caribbean in winters.

Tom, one of our club founders and a successful computer software engineer as well as a scuba diving instructor, now regains his usual composition, his smart dark eyes sparkling. "I was going to tell you here, but you are all just focused on sucking beers and eating unhealthy stuff like this pickled sausage which Dan can't stop devouring!" he exclaims with his typical witty and slightly nerdy grin.

Yes, I am thoroughly enjoying my *utopenec*, a thick sausage which is pickled in vinegar and spices with an amazing taste as well as questionable nutritional value.

"Don't pick on me, buddy, much better my sausage than your bread with lard and onion," I say, mouth full and laughing at the same time, which obviously results in spitting sausage on the table. I like Tom, he is a great friend and a very thoughtful person one can rely on.

"Let's get back to the news, folks," exclaims Zack. Another club founder, a big and tall fellow, and a computer engineer too. No one is surprised by his reaction as we all know he is a matter-of-fact guy with a very 'specific' sense of humour. "I would like to know more, one week on *Domani* sounds wonderful."

"Yes, yes, yes, tell us more, Pike," shouts everyone around the table, which makes guests sitting close by turn their heads, but they go quickly back to focusing on their beers and conversations.

Pike waits for the noise to die down and explains more. "I have one week gap between the two trips already booked, from the seventh until the fourteenth of September. It's my pleasure to dive and sail with you guys, you are a good bunch of friends. Well, I thought, and…"—he glances at Tom who was sitting on his left—"…as I told Tom, you can have a week with me at costs. Who is in?"

More cheers, more chatter. Everyone seems to be excited about the news and ready to join.

Roman, who is sitting on the opposite side of the table from me, scratches his bald head and raises his hand like at school. "Guys, I won't have a car available as I usually do, my girlfriend will be using it." We often rely on him driving, partly because he is a good driver and partly because he sometimes pays for the gas and doesn't ask for contributions from others. He is a lovely guy who is always kind. He inherited a couple of houses and now lives happily from the rent. Not bad one could say; we all like him and envy his lifestyle.

"No worries, we can use my company car and then we need just one more vehicle," I contribute to the conversation. I am a member of the board of one of the big multi-national companies in Czech Republic and can use my company car for any private trips.

"Yeah, we will sort it out, gents, don't worry," jumps in Tom, "Once we know that we can fill the boat, travel will be easy to handle. Who is in?"

Everyone raises their hand, like at school again. Even Pete, our young new member that I don't know that well. He has just finished his scuba diving course with Zack and Tom. He's committed, that's for sure.

"What about Veronika," I ask, "she usually likes to join trips like this one?"

"Hmmm, I don't know," replies Tom, "let me check with her, but she might be busy with her new job."

"We are going to *Hrvatska*, to sail and scuba dive again!" I say.

The excitement around the table is palpable. One can almost touch it. Everyone is cheerful, and we order more beers and start making plans.

The only person who has not said much yet is Michael, quietly sitting next to me and sipping his beer. He is an introverted, thoughtful person, another one who does not miss any chance to go scuba diving. Very often he and I form a buddy team.

"Michael, what do you think? You never say anything!" I tease him. He knows I mean well, so he keeps smiling with a sparkly glint in his eyes. "Of course, I am joining, what do you think? Can't miss such an opportunity for excellent scuba diving around the beautiful Dalmatian coast. Not just diving, camaraderie and nice food too."

Everyone turns to Michael with a surprised look; this was the longest speech we had heard from him for a long time.

Prague, Hloubětín
August 2002

I can't believe how lucky I am. The thought crosses my mind again. To have such a beautiful, intelligent, and passionate girlfriend like Jarka. Our deep conversations. Our amazing sex. Our wild trips around Prague's famous clubs. Life is wonderful.

I also can't believe how stupid I am, not being able to part ways with my previous girlfriend. She is sweet, but our relationship has clearly gone beyond the point of exhaustion. Still, since Jarka and I met – in a Prague club, drinking tequila and dancing on the table – I have not been able to decide what to do.

Quite an unusual situation for me, not being able to decide. I feel even more stupid because of the debate in my own head.

Stay with the 'proven' person, plan the family – a little boring but at least we know each other well?

Go for the new girl, who is such an amazing yet uncontrollable force of passion, trust my instinct and change everything?

It has been a rough couple of months, with me swaying between the two options and driving both women crazy as a result.

But today is the day. I have decided. Our club is going to leave for a scuba trip to Croatia next week, and I don't want this whole thing to keep hanging. Two hours ago, I told my now-former girl, "I am sorry, that's it, our relationship is over." She was devastated but what can I do? Now, Jarka and I lie in bed, her cat, Oskar, purring right next to our naked bodies, and I hear myself saying, "It's done, my little fox. I have told my ex that she will never see me again. I love you so much."

Jarka does not really trust me, as I said before, nevertheless she hugs me firmly, brings our bodies closer to each other and whispers into my ear:

"Let's see, you bastard. I love you too."

Prague, Karlín
September 2002

Sitting in my office in one of the cool, up-and-coming Prague districts feels very good. Our building is a super-modern office, made of glass and steel, with all the latest technology inside. Such buildings did not exist in this country even ten years ago. The company I work for is one of the most successful international conglomerates that invested in the Czech Republic early, just after the velvet revolution.

Somehow, I have managed by a mixture of hard work, good luck and, I like to think, some competency and brain power to get into the board of directors. I often work long hours, responsibilities are high, and projects and decisions are complex, but I enjoy the thrill and the pay is good.

Despite being at work and people waiting outside the office for a scheduled meeting, my mind is focused on something completely different now.

"I am sorry, guys, we must reschedule to tomorrow, I have an emergency here. Please check with my assistant for other options."

It feels strange and uncomfortable to tell them that, but I do it anyway and close the door. *Let me think.* Tom just called me this morning to tell me that one of the divers won't be able to make it. We are now six instead of the agreed seven people. What a mess! Not so much for me, I can afford to pay a little extra, but many of my friends can't, and with one person less the trip may become impossible for them. Tom told me that he already checked with all the divers in his wide network, and no one is available on such a short notice. And we are leaving in two days!

Let me think. I can't have a business meeting about the upcoming instant soups launch now.

Who can join us at the last minute? Who is flexible enough? Who has money? Who likes sailing and/or diving? Who trusts me enough that he will go even if he has never met the other guys? An almost impossible combination.

My brain starts to spin, but as one of my mottos is 'anything is possible', I won't give up until I come up with a solution.

After fifteen minutes of thinking, sifting through my memory and contact list, still nothing. When I almost give up, I think… *What about Ivo?! How could I forget about him?* My friend from the previous agency job; smart guy, fun to be around, fast decision maker, he can't dive because of his ear problems but he loves sailing. Let's give it a go! Calling now…

"Hey, Ivo, how is your life, buddy?"

"All good, little too much work, some cycling trips in the pipeline, all good. What's up?"

"Listen, you know I am in that scuba diving club. We are going to sail and dive in Croatia. The day after tomorrow." I move straight to the point. "We've got space for one more person."

"Wow, cool. I love sailing. Can't dive though, if you remember, my ears always hurt."

"Would you be able to join at such short notice?"

"Let me quickly check my agenda…"

I stay silent. Ivo is a matter-of-fact guy, ready for any adventure. If he can make it, he will.

"Yeah, there are some meetings next week, of course. Good news: nothing that can't wait. Much better to sail than to sit in the office!"

I knew it. Ivo is the man. "So, are you in?"

"Of course, buddy, I look forward to it! I have to go now, please send me some info by email or text, OK?"

"Sure thing. Take care and see you in two days!"

While hanging up, this feeling of desperation just minutes ago changes into euphoria. We are going! I decide to call Tom to tell him the good news so that he can inform the others. We are seven again.

Ivo does not know yet that this trip will be one of the most memorable experiences of his life. Of all our lives.

Prague, Krč
6th of September 2002

Shit. We are leaving in a couple of hours, and I still need to pack all the scuba gear stored in my parents' cellar. Shit, shit, shit. Work has been crazy these last couple of weeks. We are launching a new range of instant soups in September, and I still can't believe that my boss let me go to Croatia. I told her it's just a week, everything is ready, the marketing and sales teams are good, everyone knows what to do. No worries, I will be back in just one short week. Well, what could she say? She let me go.

Then all the girlfriend's stuff. Oh my god! What a mess. I am happy that I finally was able to decide (really?) and sort it out. Even though sometimes it feels like being alone, independent, free, and just having occasional sex with some random women is an attractive option. Sadly, it's not my style and I envy some of my friends who are able to live life like this. I love relationships, depth, and the feeling of two people trusting each other. Well, that's it then. Forget about it and focus on the bloody packing!

Here is the large blue nylon bag, 5mm double-piece wetsuit – the Mediterranean Sea can be quite cold even in summer – hoodie, regulator, spare regulator, BCD, two masks, dive computer, compass, fins, boots, logbook… what else? What else?! Oh, gloves, I nearly forgot. Neoprene gloves and a few surgical gloves too as an additional insulation layer as my hands easily get cold. All good, I got it. One hour to go, my friends will pick me up here. Everything is done even though it was all last minute as always.

The adrenaline injected into my bloodstream by the time-stressed brain is slowly being flushed out of the body. Instead, a calm yet vibrant expectation of the trip is taking over, imagining all the beautiful sailing, time with friends, tasty Mediterranean food, and underwater experiences that we will enjoy in Croatia together. I have no idea, of course, that reality will surpass even the wildest possible expectations.

Friends are already here. I will drive with Zack and Michael, and Ivo will join us in a small town in Morava where his parents live. We have all the equipment and, most importantly, lots of beer and wine, which no scuba diving trip will work without. Czechs are famous for bringing their own cheap booze to Croatia instead of buying locally.

The road trip is long but fun. Everyone takes his turn driving – except for Michael who just sleeps the whole time.

Croatia, Split
7th of September 2002

The atmosphere is ecstatic. Our group of divers, sailors, and to-be explorers has arrived after a long car journey from Prague to the Split port, in one of the most beautiful towns on the Croatian coast in the Dalmatian region. We have just boarded the sailboat which will serve as our floating home for the next seven days. Captain Pike has already assigned the double cabins, everyone has off-loaded their gear, and we are sitting in the salon, eating lovely local white bread with olive oil and fried calamari. What a treat!

Pike pulls out the nautical chart and we start discussing our journey. Where should we sail? What is interesting in the area? How is the weather forecast? Everyone speaks at the same time, that's how excited the whole group is. Pike, with his usual calm presence, asks for a moment of silence and shows us his ideas.

"We can sail around the islands Brač and Hvar, visit Šolta island, scuba dive at many different localities, visit the abandoned submarine base from the second world war, anchor in small, beautiful bays for nights, log in a couple of night dives, explore some of the islands by foot and finish in Split again, to enjoy one of the mediaeval gems in the Dalmatian coast at the end of our trip. Sounds good?"

Everyone is cheering and clapping, already imagining what's ahead of us.

Sails up!

Island Brač
8th of September 2002

First day of scuba diving! It starts with a shipwreck near the island Mrduja, followed by Brač with an amazing cave called Lučica. I usually dive with Roman; he is calm. We just enjoy the underwater atmosphere. Zack buddies up with Michael and Tom with our greenhorn Pete as Tom is the most experienced diver of the whole group. He just finished the GUE Tech 1 course and is simply the best. Our captain, 'Lazy bugger', we say, claims that he is an old and sick person and therefore can't dive. I think he just wants to lie on the deck and relax.

Tonight, we anchor in one of the abandoned bays of Brač, where the water is so beautiful and calm. We don't miss women (perhaps yet). Boys' trips are so much fun – we can fart as we please and talk utter nonsense.

Island Hvar
9th of September 2002

Today, we are sailing to Hvar! The first dive is under the Kabal lighthouse. Ivo is lazy too – he does not want to try scuba, complaining that his ears hurt when underwater. He should at least try it! Obviously, he won't, at least not on this trip.

In the evening, we arrive at the Hvar town, moor at the pier, and walk to the centre for some nice Croatian fish with a couple of glasses of local wine. We are all so tired from the whole day of diving and sunbathing that we go back to the boat rather soon. Ivo sleeps in our cabin, while I always sleep on the deck. At least when the weather is nice, which is often the case in summer here. Sleeping outdoors on the boat remains one of my favourite experiences in life. One can see all the stars, hear the ocean splashing, feel the boat rock gently from side to side…

Island Velki Vodnjak
10th of September 2002

After a couple days of sailing and diving we are all adjusted to life at sea. We take turns in cooking food, even though of course some people are preferred chefs thanks to their skills, while others are barely tolerated; that's how you know if men cook at home or let their wives and girlfriends do everything!

Everyone is happy, and boat life is relatively simple and straightforward: wake up, dive, breakfast, swim, sail, lunch, dive, chill, swim, dinner, go to bed. We often gather at the salon or cockpit around a meal and that's the time for sharing life stories, discussing our recent dives, and contemplating our upcoming plan.

Even my friend Ivo who joined at the last minute and shares a cabin with me seems really happy, just enjoying sailing, sea, the simplicity of everything, reading his books, and the company of people which he did not know before the trip but has found to be a rather amusing group of characters. He must be thinking *How come all these guys are so excited about being underwater with all this complicated equipment?*

We just finished an amazing dive on the vertical wall of Vodnjak island, my deepest dive ever! I was with Roman and Tom, at 52 metres, looking at the massive gorgonian coral fans, beautiful red corals, huge sponges, and a couple of large fish. It felt a bit strange to be so deep; it was only my 107th dive, but I know that I can rely on the experience of Tom, who doesn't even know how many dives he has done – he estimates around 5,000. Even though I had nitrogen narcosis, for sure, my heartbeat felt like a gargantuan bell ringing inside my chest.

Now we are sitting around the salon table. Pike pulls out the nautical chart – some people incorrectly call it a 'map' – of the Dalmatian coast and shows us our next plan. He wants to move to the southern coast of Šolta island where there are several sheltered bays where we can anchor during the night, protected from any swell and wind. Possibly, we can go for our first night dive of the trip as those bays are usually calm and shallow – ideal conditions for a night dive.

Everyone looks at the chart, nodding. It sounds like a good plan. Michael points at one of the bays called Uvala Poganica and asks Pike what this small circle drawn by hand on the chart is. Pike explains that he was there with another group recently. They were sailing and snorkelling and found a dark hole in the seabed at around 10 metres' depth. He has no idea what's there, perhaps just a shallow cavern. They did not explore it as his guests were not divers, so he just marked it on the chart to remember and find out more on some of the future trips. Energy around the table immediately shifts, from calm listening to excited chatter. It's obvious that we simply must explore this secret spot!

Pike puts the chart back inside the navigation table, nods, and moves to the front of the boat to pull up the anchor.

Let's sail to Šolta.

Island Šolta, Poganica Bay
10th of September 2002, 17:00

The whole group is sitting around the cockpit table, enjoying the afternoon sun as well as a salad with grilled fresh tuna prepared by Pike, plus famous Croatian soft bread. We arrived at the Poganica bay and anchored close to one of the shores, protected from three sides by the island hills. There is another sailboat with a German crew anchored here, but the bay is quite large. We both have enough space. A light afternoon breeze gently swings our boat. There are almost no waves – perfect conditions for a night dive. Everyone is looking forward to the dive as well as to a calm night on board.

I fish out my SLR camera and take a couple of portrait pictures: Tom with his funny grin and even funnier hat; Zack who does not want to be photographed; Pike whose eyes are slowly getting very narrow at this time of the day, usually he is fast asleep by 7pm; Michael smiling to the camera, enjoying the few last bites of the tuna salad.

Everyone is getting ready for the night dive, pulling out scuba tanks from the lockers. Captain is already lying flat on the salon sofa, and Ivo retreated to the front of the boat to make space for all the manipulation with scuba gear. Not easy on a small sailing boat! I won't dive as I feel cold. This is my usual problem – unless the temperature is above 25°C, my body, having a limited amount of fat, cools down, therefore night dives are often not my cup of tea.

Our anchorage point is around 30 metres from where we think the hole is in the sea floor. Four divers – Tom, Zack, Roman, and Pete – are ready to jump. Michael does not feel like diving again too, but he takes his mask, fins, and snorkel to accompany the divers from the surface to see what they can find. The black hole may be just a shallow cavern – nothing interesting. If there is anything cool, we will have plenty of time tomorrow to explore more.

Darkness slowly descends on the bay while divers empty their BCDs and submerge. My watch shows 20:05. Michael swims away from the boat together with them, his fins rhythmically splashing water and the sound echoing from the surrounding bay hills. I start reading my book, covering myself with the blanket, looking forward to hearing about what the divers found.

I am barely a couple of pages into the book when Michael pops up next to the boat and starts briskly climbing the ladder, his eyes full of sparks.

"It's a cave, it's a cave!" he shouts. "The guys went inside and haven't come back for at least five minutes! It must be an underwater cave. I can't miss it and will join them. Will you join too?"

I really don't feel like diving, so Michael quickly kits up, hurriedly getting into his wetsuit. His tank, BCD, and regulator are ready.

"Don't worry," he says, "I won't be alone, will join them."

The divers are very close to the boat somewhere in the hole. If he joins them they can explore together and continue with the night dive after looking at the cave. Even though it crosses my mind that one of the principal rules of scuba diving says that a diver should never dive alone, in this situation it's probably OK, I think. He will join them in a couple of minutes. Off he goes and I get back to my book.

Oh, let's not forget to text my love, Jarka. We got used to texting each other a brief message each evening:

"I love you, fox."

"I love you too" flies back all the way from Prague.

Island Šolta, Poganica Bay
10th of September 2002, 21:05

A calm night has already descended on the Poganica bay, stars glitter in the dark blue sky, the evening breeze dies down. So peaceful, so beautiful. The calm before the storm.

Bubbles start popping up around the boat, and the divers are returning from the night dive. They immersed a diving light under the boat so that they could easily find their way back. I put my book aside, curious to hear what they have found. The boat ladder is narrow; they have to climb one at a time. Slowly, they fill out the cockpit at the back of the boat and start taking their masks off, immediately getting into an animated discussion.

Zack: "Did you see that?!"

Roman: "What a complex underwater cave! Pity I didn't have the courage to go further."

Pete: "So many corridors after that chimney down. Not my cup of tea, boys."

Zack: "OMG, we have to explore more tomorrow but we don't have the right cave diving gear here."

Roman: "Glad that we turned around, it's not a great idea to explore an unknown underwater cave on a night dive…"

Tom, the only experienced cave diver among us: "Yes, sorry, guys, I had to turn around, we didn't have any lines, only single tanks, none of you are trained for cave diving, the silt attached to the ceiling started falling down and messed up the visibility. Excuse me for chickening out, but we had to turn."

Pete: "No worries, you did the right thing, Tom, absolutely the right thing."

Me: "Where is Michael?"

Island Šolta, Poganica Bay
10th of September 2002, 21:10

"*What?*"

Everyone turns towards me. All the chatter immediately stops like if you drop an f-bomb during a wedding dinner, and everyone stares at me and tries to process my question.

"We did not see him. He went snorkelling, we descended into the cave and when we got back out, Michael wasn't around, we continued our dive around the sloping wall of the bay. Last time we saw him was on the surface before we entered the hole."

Everybody senses that something is not right. By now, both Ivo and Captain Pike are here too, all of us crammed into the small space at the stern.

"Let me explain," I say, my tone of voice revealing my worries. "Michael came back to the boat several minutes after he apparently saw from the water surface that all of you were going down into the black hole, put on his scuba gear quickly, saying he will join the group, explore together with you. He left the boat around one hour ago. He must have absolutely trusted that he was joining you folks."

Tom cannot believe his ears. "Oh my god, if he got into that cave, it's a mess. Big mess. The place is rather complex, we don't know how complex, we just peeked in and turned around when I realized that it's dangerous to go further during the night, without proper equipment, solid lights, lines and so on. Also, none of you guys is a trained cave diver, I am sorry. It was my responsibility as a cave diving instructor to evaluate the situation and stop there. So, we ascended back to the entrance at the depth of ten metres, checked on each other and agreed underwater to continue the night dive around the bay. None of us has seen Michael, right, guys?"

Everyone nods. All the faces are immediately very serious. *What if he really is in the cave? What do we do now?* Our brains are not willing to accept what our imaginations are suggesting.

One thing is clear: Michael is lost, either in the cave or somewhere in the bay and there is darkness all around, not just inside of the cave. Another thing is clear: we must find him. Fast. Because… he is already running out of air.

Island Šolta, Poganica Bay
10th of September 2002, 21:20

Everyone speaks at the same time, before Tom, with his calm authority, asks for a moment of silence and starts to lay out his ideas for the rescue operation. It's obvious that we are Michael's only chance – no one from the Croatian Coast Guard will come in the middle of the night to this remote island, and for sure they won't dive into the cave. Michael trusted the group to the point that he went alone on a dive thinking that he would join them. Now, we must trust our instincts, our reasoning, and our capabilities to save him, wherever he is.

We stand inside the salon. From the back of the boat, we can hear the compressor rattle, as Pike had already started to fill the empty scuba tanks.

Tom starts to lead our rescue efforts. "Zack, Roman with Pike, take the zodiac and a couple of torches. You can thoroughly search around the entire bay. If Michael *is not* in the cave, sitting somewhere on the shore rocks, you will find him."

Zack jumps straight in. "Sounds good to me, let's get ready. But… who will go into the cave? All the divers had just finished a long, even though shallow, dive and won't be able to dive right away without risking the deco sickness."

"Unfortunately, I have to go," Tom responds without hesitation. "I am the only person here with solid cave diving experience, more than two thousand dives. There is no other way."

"I can join you," I hear myself saying without really knowing what it means to dive in such an underwater cave.

"Dan," Tom says, "I appreciate you stepping up, but you have never been in a cave before. I am sorry but you might be more of a problem than help. I won't be able to focus on the search *and* taking care of you."

"You are right, Tom. Still, how can I help? I haven't been diving, I can stay underwater for much longer than any of you."

"Why don't you take a few spare tanks and wait at the cave entrance, at ten metre depth? If I find Michael, he will have a serious deco penalty, he must stay underwater to get rid of all the nitrogen dissolved in his body. I will get a long deco stop too. If you are there and help us, that would be great."

"Sure thing, Tom, I am ready." My voice is firm, but my hands are shaking a bit. *Will our plan work?* It must!

While I am kitting up, Tom shares his limited knowledge of the cave architecture. "The entrance is ten metres deep, an elliptic hole in rough diameter of two metres, followed by a vertical chimney down to around twenty-two metres' depth where the cave appears to have several chambers or corridors heading into various directions. That's where we stopped and turned around during the first ascent."

"Do you think that he might have ventured further?" asks Roman, his voice trembling.

"Well… we don't know," Tom replies, calmly but with a very serious face. "One can only hope that Michael did not swim too far from the entrance and that the visibility from the falling silt attached to the ceiling is not too bad."

"What if he is out of air already?!" jumps in Pete, our novice, panic in his voice. He for sure did not expect such a turn of events.

Tom tries to take away the drama from the situation before it escalates and infects the others. "Pete, let's calm down. Anxiety won't help us now and won't help Michael either. We all understand that the situation is critical. That's why we must stay focused, do what we can. Perhaps there is another exit from the cave, or he found an air pocket where he can breathe even if his tank got empty already."

"Let's go, guys, as agreed and good luck." My leadership instinct now replaces the fear. I know that in such moments, one has to stay calm and steady, not allowing people to get paralyzed by worries.

The zodiac team is waiting for us in the dinghy. The tanks are ready, and Tom and I jump in and off we go, just a short ride to position ourselves on top of the cave entrance. We switch on our diving lights, don't waste any time with the usual obligatory buddy check, roll back into the water, and immediately start descending to the cave entrance. The display on my dive computer shows 21:40. I hear the boat engine roaring up as the search team departs to their ride around the bay.

The darkness beckons. The cave entrance is fast approaching, and I equalize my ears by pinching my nose and moving my tongue up, the Frenzel manoeuvre usually used by freedivers. The black hole is surrounded by a rather uninteresting seabed. *Where is Michael? How is this whole thing going to end up?*

Tom signals a usual dive 'OK' with thumb and index finger connected to form an 'o'. I respond in the same way and look into his eyes. There is determination and calm and, at the same time, a hint of fear. Fear of what's coming. *Is he going to find Michael? Alive or already out of air and dead?* No one knows, but both of us think the same, without verbalizing it.

Tom ties the improvised line to the nearby rock, exhales a bunch of bubbles, and starts his descent into the cave. I station myself lying flat on the ridge of the cave, full of expectations and thousands of good luck wishes, seeing his silhouette. It's surrounded by light from the diving torch and slowly disappears into the darkness. I can't see him any longer, but his bubbles still keep floating up to the surface for some time but after several minutes stop. He must be inside of the cave corridors, his exhaled air getting trapped under the ceiling, further worsening visibility in the cave.

I am alone now, in the middle of the night, looking into the abyss. Silence here is profound, except for my own breath. Sucking air slowly in from the regulator and expelling bubbles with their typical bubbly sound. *What would you call the sound that bubbles make?*

My thoughts keep flowing, in some kind of slow motion. Tom is the most experienced and trustworthy diver I have ever met. If there is someone who can find Michael, it's him. But… the time is for sure up. If Michael is in the cave, he is either out of air or facing a serious decompression penalty before he can ascend. The nearest decompression chamber is in Split, if it is open so late in the night. He might be hiding in an unlikely air pocket desperately waiting for someone to find him. Possibly there is another exit from the cave and Michael is somewhere on the beach, waving at our rubber boat to pick him up.

I am definitely not the most religious person; nevertheless, I find myself almost praying for him to be somewhere other than down there. If he is there, his chances for survival are extremely limited.

Those and many more ideas are circling in my mind as I am waiting and waiting and waiting for Tom (and hopefully Michael too!) to come back. Tom's scuba tank has 15 litres of air, which could give him around an hour of dive time, obviously depending on the dive depth. However, he has already been on another dive just before this one, so he can't stay too long at the depth below 20 metres as he will quickly collect a decompression stop obligation. I try to save my air. Even though there is another full scuba tank lying next to me, we might need all the air there is if he comes back with Michael, and they must stay for a long deco stop.

Time passes very slowly. Despite the situation being crazy serious, I find myself calm, almost serene, being on my own in the ocean, in the dark, staring intently into the cave chimney. Inhale, exhale. Check time. Inhale, exhale. The only other sound that one can hear here is perhaps a very light cracking of small waves that are washing the shore nearby above me. *This is going to be one of the longest hours of my life,* I think to myself.

Island Šolta, Poganica Bay
10th of September 2002, 22:20

My dive computer shows that we are already 40' into the dive.

Tom's time must be soon up. I hope he is coming back! What if not???

My mind takes me back to the moment on the boat. Tom and I were discussing the best possible course of action to find Michael.

"What's your plan, Tom?"

"The cave seems quite complex, and I don't have a proper reel. On top of that, it can go deep. Under normal circumstances, it could be a fantastic exploration. Tonight, it's a mess, and we don't have much time to find him."

"Yes, it's a mess. Listen, buddy, you are a cave diving instructor, I know. But this would be your third dive today. Decompression and everything. Please take care. The most important thing is not to risk your life. Michael might be still alive. Or not. We don't know."

"Sure, I will be careful. I will give it a shot, there is nothing else to do. We need to at least try. I will be back in thirty, max forty minutes, to manage the decompression."

"All right. I will be waiting at the entrance with full tanks for you. Hopefully for him too."

"Yes. Perfect. But listen to me carefully. Under no circumstances should you even think about following me down. If you had proper training – no problem. You don't. Cave can be a bitch. If I don't come up after sixty minutes, I am lost too. It won't happen, but just in case. You will pack everything and get back to the boat. Agreed?" He glanced at me with an intense, piercing look.

"Well… agreed. Come back, all right!"

What if he does not come back? What do I do? Go down to find him?

He explicitly told me not to dive into the cave.

Will I find the strength to just surface without trying to help?

My calmness gives way to anxiety, and I notice that my breathing becomes faster.

Calm down, stupid! We will need the air.

Bubbles of air hit my mask, and I realize that Tom must be exiting the cave corridors and starting his ascent through the vertical chimney towards the entrance. Here, his silhouette appears again in the depths below me, surrounded by faint light as his dive torch is slowly running out of batteries. He is alone.

When he ascends out of the cave, our eyes meet. We can't speak, but no words are necessary. He shakes his head.

Michael is either still there, by now for sure out of air and dead, or hopefully somewhere outside, already found by our friends. Perhaps he is already back at the boat, celebrating his rescue with an obligatory beer and telling the story to the others. We will soon find out.

For now, we must wait as Tom has an agonizing 30-minute-long decompression stop at three to six metres of depth. He switches to the full scuba tank which I was holding for Michael as his air supply is at this moment almost exhausted. He has been there as long as humanly possible.

Tom and I are side by side now, hovering above the black cave mouth, slowly breathing, waiting for the deco stop to finish.

When his dive watch shows zero decompression time, we look at each other and ascend slowly to the surface together.

Island Šolta, Poganica Bay
10th of September 2002, 22:55

Our rubber boat is nowhere to be seen, so Tom and I are slowly swimming on our backs to the boat.

"Have you found him?" shouts someone while we are still in the water, taking off our fins. This means that he is obviously lost.

Shit. Shit, shit, shit. Now the small spark of hope is gone. We hear the boat engine getting closer; our search team is coming back too. No Michael on board. We take off our gear and gather in the yacht salon. This is going to be one of the longest nights of our lives. What to do now?

Captain is clear: "We must call the coast guard boys. We have done everything possible and now we simply have to inform the authorities otherwise we are in trouble."

He picks up his phone and calls the emergency line. Everyone else stays silent, waiting for the outcome. Perhaps Croatians have some kind of search and rescue team ready for situations like this? Perhaps they can search the surrounding bays better than us in a small rubber dinghy? Captain clearly explains our situation, our position, and then listens. "No, you have to come now, we have one diver lost!" we hear him shouting – not typical of him – to the speaker.

He hangs up and turns to the group. "They are coming tomorrow morning. Nothing to be done during the night."

If Michael is still alive somewhere down there, his chances are almost nil now.

What should we do next? We start discussing again but there is not much else we can do. Our dinghy search group rode several times around the bay and surrounding area, but found nothing.

The possibilities are clear:

1. If Michael is in the cave, by now he is for sure out of air and his dive light battery is gone. He is dead.

2. If he is in the cave and found an air pocket, he can still survive depending on how big the air pocket is before he consumes all the oxygen there. There is no way he can find the way out as his scuba tank must be empty. Hopefully, the Croatian rescue team will know the cave layout and be able to find him tomorrow.

3. If he is not in the cave, he must have gotten lost somewhere at sea. We must wait for sunrise and then we'll explore the island's shores again. That would be the best outcome – he will have to spend the night outside; not great, but survival is still possible as the temperature won't drop below 18°C. There are no strong currents here, hence the probability that he was swept away to the open ocean is very low.

“Let’s call our cave diving friends back home,” suggests someone. “Perhaps they know more about this cave.”

Tom agrees that this is a good idea. Czech cave divers are some of the best in Europe. Everyone feels very helpless and desperate to do something instead of just waiting for the day to come. We start contacting whoever we know but after an hour it is clear that no one knows anything. We found an unknown, complex underwater cave, went exploring it at night, and one of us most probably got lost there. What a mess.

Everyone slowly retreats to their cabins. Not much else we can do. I stay on the deck, looking at the stars and wishing Michael good luck. *If he is still there, he will need it.* A sleepless night and nervous silence descend on our sailboat. There is beautiful nature all around us. This could have been one of the most serene evenings of our trip. Instead, we are in a nightmare. On top of that, I feel guilty for asking Ivo, my good, non-diving friend, to join us, but of course no one could have predicted what would happen tonight.

Oops, I nearly forgot about my love! A quick text message, “I love you and thinking of you”, flies to Prague. She does not need to know about our situation here and get worried. Not yet.

Island Šolta and back to Split
11th of September 2002

Nobody had a good sleep, obviously. The adrenaline rush of last night has evaporated and now we all are a bit apathetic, tired, and we are not sure what else can be done. Breakfast is prepared and everyone eats their bread and cheese in silence. In any case, we must wait for the Croatian Coast Guard to arrive from Split and then we'll see. The German sailboat is nowhere to be seen. They probably left early in the morning. It is incredible to think they had no idea what kind of drama was happening underwater while they slept.

Here they are! A medium-sized white powerboat of the Croatian Coast Guard appears at the bay entrance and rounds the bend, still riding full throttle. In a minute it is next to us, slows down, and lands near the starboard (that's what sailors call the right side) of our sailboat. We see four people on board: a skipper behind the steering wheel, two young-looking guys in camouflage uniforms, probably army or police divers, and another man in civil clothes who seems to be giving orders.

The commander stays on the coast guard boat, and we start talking. Luckily, Czech and Croatian languages are somewhat similar, therefore we can understand each other. Our captain Pike explains the situation and the whole drama of the previous night and points to the calm surface of the sea not far from our anchored boats where we know the cave entrance is. The commander nods and says something to the young guys. They start kitting up into wetsuits and preparing their scuba gear. But something is clearly not right. They only have single tanks and single regulators. We don't see gear mandatory for cave explorations. No helmets, no lights, no reels, no lines, no spools, no double tanks… *Oh my god, it's clear that these guys have no idea what they are getting into!*

Tom now jumps into a conversation between our captain and the coast guard commander while the divers are getting ready.

"Excuse me, sir," he says, "but this is a serious, potentially complex cave system. With all respect, your divers don't appear to have the equipment required for such an undertaking."

Tom uses his most polite tone of voice and tries to remain calm. However, it's visible that he is very concerned. "What is their experience and training in cave diving, please?"

The commander brushes his question away with a wave of his hand: "No worries, folks, our divers are from the Croatian Navy, they will sort out everything, *nema problema*."

We all look at each other, not believing what we hear. This is very serious. We all have some basic understanding of cave diving risks and thorough training with special gear required to at least minimize those risks. Tom is the only one with a lot of practice and many dives in various caves around Europe and the US.

He just shakes his head with disbelief and tries to convince the commander again: "Sir, it is my duty as a cave diving instructor to warn you, this cave is potentially dangerous, and your team does not appear to have the necessary equipment…"

The commander interrupts him briskly, now with an impatient tone of voice: "Don't worry. Let's stop this discussion. We are in charge here and our divers are the best. We will go and find your friend, wherever he is, dead or alive. Now, if you have any spare diving lights, give them to our divers."

Further attempts to convince him about the foolishness of the plan would clearly be futile. We collect a couple of scuba torches and hand them over the railing to the two navy divers who are now ready to go. The commander speaks to the skipper; the boat moves away from us and slowly approaches the indicated location of the cave entrance. The divers roll back into the water and disappear. All of us are tense, even more than last night.

I hope these divers will survive.

When we look at the water surface with the cave entrance underneath, there are bubbles still coming up. Strange. If both navy divers descended into the cave, the bubbles should now be trapped against the cave ceiling. It could only mean that one of the divers went inside and the other is waiting at the entrance. How are they going to manage it? How are they going to help each other? What if they find Michael. How is one diver going to bring him up? Too many questions and no answers.

Finally, one of the longest hours of our lives is over. Now they must be coming back any moment because their scuba tanks will soon be empty. It is weird to only see one stream of bubbles breaching the surface.

One diver is still at the entrance, but where is the other?

By now he should be at his safety deco stop at around six metres' depth! But we continue to see one stream of bubbles only. The commander of the police boat seems to be getting more nervous as well.

Tom and I look at each other and understand without words.

Another diver is most likely lost! No. No, no, no! What a mess!

I catch myself nodding and start getting into my wetsuit. Tom too. Our friends' eyes are wide and afraid.

"What are you two doing?" asks Zack.

"Guys, the navy diver is probably lost too. We must help him," replies Tom.

"Yes, let's try the same thing as last night," I add, shaking my head in disbelief.

There is some commotion in the water. One of the divers breaches the surface, spits the regulator out of his mouth, and immediately starts shouting at his boss. We don't understand the words but it's more than clear that he is stressed.

The coast guard boat quickly approaches and stops next to our sailboat. Tom and I are ready.

"Our diver is gone! Our diver didn't come back!" shouts the commander, now clearly panicking.

"Yes, we understand, we will try to find him," replies Tom with a quiet but trembling voice.

"OK, good luck, please find him fast, we have no other option." The commander blesses our rescue operation and off we go.

Tom shows OK with his thumb and index finger yet again. I reply the same and we empty our BCDs. Another dive into the damned cave. Even though no one can blame the cave, it's been here watching stupid humans probably for thousands of years…

We descend to the ledge around the entrance, back to the black hole again. No more communication is required, no more plans necessary. We are going to attempt the same dive as last night. Tom ties the improvised line around the big rock next to the hole, switches on his diving light, exhales, and begins to descend. I lie on the edge, another spare air tank right next to me lying on the rocks. I keep peering into the darkness, seeing Tom's silhouette disappear again. Déjà vu.

There is no more hope of finding Michael alive. Maybe Tom can find his body. Maybe he can find the navy diver, we learned that his name is Olan. I trust Tom's abilities and skills, the calm judgement to do the utmost to find the missing diver, but mostly I hope that he himself will come back.

I want to shout at the cave "STOP IT! ENOUGH!!!", but the cry stays in my mind.

There is no point in shouting at the creation of nature. Nobody forced our group to go down and explore. Nobody told Michael to dive alone.

With the navy divers, the situation is of course different. They came to rescue our friend, and their leader told them to dive. Despite our warnings. What a mess again.

I stare into the dark black hole just in front of me. Unlike last night, sun rays are penetrating the surface now, reaching into the depths and flickering with every little wave above me.

Quite a beautiful sight, I am thinking, not being able to stop admiring the ocean around me regardless of how desperate our situation is.

Tom appears in the depths below me sooner than I expected.

What happened? Has he found anyone?

Only his bubbles are rising to the surface, and I know that he has not been able to discover any of the missing divers. He ascends next to me to the cave entrance, shakes his head, and waves his hand in front of his mask. Oh my, the visibility in the cave got really bad – Tom later talks about how you couldn't see past 20cm; one couldn't even see his own dive watch – as the divers stirred even more silt attached to the walls and the ceiling. It's clear that any rescue operation won't be possible until the silt slowly sinks to the bottom. This almost certainly means that the two divers are now dead.

Tom and I ascend to the surface and immediately face the impatient commander.

"Nothing???" he asks, as if it was not clear.

Tom replies, still in the water: "Unfortunately nothing, I am sorry. The visibility is non-existent, we don't have proper equipment, no backup divers. You better call some real cave diving experts, otherwise there is no chance."

The commander disappears inside the boat cockpit; we hear a VHF radio cracking and his voice urgently explaining the situation to someone at the other end. Then their boat suddenly powers up and leaves without any explanation.

Tom and I swim to our boat, climb the ladder, take off our gear, and immediately start discussing with the rest of the crew. Now we are in an even more serious mess. Two divers are missing, one of them being a local navy diver. One who came to rescue our friend.

What does it matter that we told them not to dive? Who cares now? What will happen next? Are we supposed to wait here?

Nobody knows.

One hour after my dive with Tom and some impatient waiting, another boat, this time with large Croatian Police signs, shows up and anchors next to us. We are told to follow them to the Maslinica harbour on the western side of Šolta island. Leaving the place without one of us feels horrible.

There we moor at the pier and wait again. Police guys sit next to the ice cream kiosk and are constantly on their cell phones. Meanwhile, the white coast guard boat arrives on the other side of the harbour. We don't see clearly what's happening there, but they seem to be picking up some men in overalls and loading scuba gear. Everything flashes by and they quickly leave without even considering talking to 'our' policemen. They run around on the shore, waving their arms and shouting, but the coast guard crew does not pay any attention and leaves the bay. Police utter a couple of swear words and go back to sitting next to the ice cream stand. One of them opens a beer can. We look at each other, clearly shocked by their relaxed approach.

After some time of painful waiting again, our two guys receive a phone call, stand up, get on to our boat, and tell us to move to the nearby capital of Dalmatian province, Split. That's where we started our journey just a couple of days ago.

Pike begins preparing the sailboat for departure and starts the engine. I move to the bow to pull up the mooring rope. Some kind of strange orange paint got onto the rope while it was attached to the pier and my shorts get all messed up while pulling it up. Well, what to do, I have another pair. The line is released, I signal to Pike, he reverses, then turns the boat around and off we go.

On the way to Split, the sea is again beautiful, but all of us have very different thoughts; we're not here to admire nature. Our friend is dead. One of the navy divers is dead. We don't know for sure but it's almost certain. No one from our crew knows what to expect.

How will this situation unfold? What are we supposed to do?

Nobody has any idea. I cry under my sunglasses as all the emotions now come and overwhelm me.

Everyone is very tired. The last evening and sleepless night start to take their toll.

There are some police guys without uniforms waiting for us at the pier in Split, telling us to jump into the prepared cars. We are driving to the police station through the historical town centre. We certainly look like tourists, with our shorts, T-shirts, and flip flops. One major difference is that not one of us is smiling, very different to crowds of foreigners who every summer flock to this mediaeval gem of a town in the Dalmatian region. Summer atmosphere is all around us. On the other side of the police car window, people are sitting in restaurants and coffee shops, eating wonderful local seafood and sipping wine or beer. No one knows why we are here and what's going through our minds.

At the police station we are told to sit down in the hall and wait. Luckily, Czech and Croatian languages are both Slavic, with similar words and structure, therefore we have no problem understanding the basics. We are called in one by one to provide our testimony on the events of the last night. The procedure is very slow, so we are rather quietly waiting for our respective turns.

Finally, all the pressure and physical activity of last night catches up with me and I struggle to keep my eyes open. My turn arrives while it is already dark outside. I explain what happened, and the officers write down my responses, asking questions from time to time. Everything seems sad but very smooth. They are used to dealing with all sorts of accidents and deaths, I guess.

I take my phone from the pocket and message my love, *Can't talk now but everything is all right,* but am interrupted by the police guy.

"You are not allowed to use your phone!" he shouts, but nevertheless doesn't make a move to take the phone from me.

"Why not?" I dare to respond. WTF?

"You are at the police station, using cell phones is only allowed when we tell you."

It doesn't make sense to argue, I guess, so I put the phone back. There will be another chance.

More waiting… nothing to do, just contemplate our situation. What's next?

After a while, around midnight, Ivo and I are asked to go into one of the offices; others are told the same. They seem to be splitting us into smaller groups.

Ivo and I found ourselves in a rather uninteresting police office, few shelves full of files covering one of the walls, a couple of tables with simple chairs around them.

"You will sleep here tonight, make yourself comfortable," says the police officer who brought us here, with a slight grin.

Sleep at the police station?! Ivo and I look at each other, not believing what we just heard.

"Excuse me, what do you mean by *sleep here*? There are no beds, nothing to lie down on."

"Well, that's what it is. Up to you." He finishes his short talk and walks out of the room.

Strange but what to do.

With no police in the room, it's time to text to my fox. She will be asleep now. How I wish to be next to her now! Instead, I sit on a chair with my head on the table, and Ivo tries to fall asleep on the floor. No cushions, no pillows, no blankets. What a night!

"What do you think?" I ask, trying to keep my voice low so that the police guy who might be outside doesn't hear us.

"I have no idea. It's a bit strange. Yes, two people are most likely dead but it's clearly an accident," replies Ivo, whispering too.

"Why do you whisper? We haven't done anything." I try to tease him to bring a bit of fun into the situation. No one is laughing though.

"I really don't know what to make of it. We told them what we know, they should let us go back to the boat."

"Sure, I mean, they can always ask us to come back tomorrow, no?"

"I am too tired to even think about it now. Let's try to sleep and make a plan in the morning. It feels like we should call the Czech consul to help us," finishes Ivo, turning around on the rather hard linoleum floor.

"I agree. Good night, if it's at all possible."

"Good night."

We are so tired that eventually both of us fall into a dreamless sleep.

Split, Criminal Police Station of Dalmatia 12th of September 2002

I have been through lots of interesting and sometimes crazy situations in my life. This Thursday will definitely become a part of the collection of the most memorable days. I don't know it yet, but I will find out soon.

A rather rude wake-up call by one of the criminalists, and a visit to the toilet accompanied by him. Ivo must go separately. A couple of sips from the tap in the bathroom. Teeth brushing nowhere in sight, oh my god.

I am being told to go with the uniformed police guy. We walk down the stairs, somewhere into the inner parts of the police station. They take our photographs. Fingerprints. I start to feel like I'm in a criminal thriller movie. They tell me that I must give my blood sample. This is another wake-up call. I refuse and ask for the Czech consul to join us. One of the police guys says that he will break my arm and there will be enough blood. *What?* I am not sure if I heard properly, so I decide to shut up and pretend that I don't understand anything.

Now a lie detector! The feeling of being in a movie changes into a much more real fear. In the lie detector room, I see our consul, Vera, which calms me down a bit. She looks very serious though. They keep asking some questions and if I am ready to take the test. I look at the consul. She nods. I agree, there is nothing to hide.

They connect me to the machine, a sleeve like when you get a blood pressure test, several springs around the chest, two wires connected to the fingers of my right hand. A stupid idea crosses my mind along the lines of *We can learn something every day* – I have always thought that lie detectors monitor brain waves. Apparently not in Croatia. They start asking questions:

"How did Michael die?"

"What happened during the night?"

"Was he strangled? Was he stabbed?"

What the hell are these questions about? I think to myself, but try to answer in the calmest manner possible. That is rather difficult though. They keep asking:

"Do you know why we ask questions about Michael's death?"

"Do you know that he was stabbed with a knife?"

"Did you know it was a murder?"

What the fuck??!! I answer negatively to all the questions, but it is very difficult to keep calm in such a situation, moreover after a couple of sleepless nights. I start shaking and become very nervous. *What kind of tricks are they playing on me?! Michael went down to the cave and most likely drowned. Murder?! Not possible.*

"What was the weapon that Michael was murdered with?"

The criminal police guy – he must be crazy! – who had said earlier that he will break my arm says that Michael was stabbed to death. I am being disconnected from the detector, I hear myself as if I was outside of my body asking about the test results. They refuse and escort me from the room. He threatens me again and makes some vulgar gestures. I decide the best strategy is to ignore him.

Another round of fingerprints. The damned paint is so difficult to remove from the fingers, it drives me nuts. They give me some dishwashing detergent, it works well. I simply don't like dirty fingers. Also, I don't like not brushing my teeth. Such simple things that we usually take for granted. But let's forget about it, it doesn't matter. What matters – I am starting to get some clear thoughts again – is that *they are trying to frame us.* I realize that I haven't seen Ivo since the morning bathroom trip and wonder how he is doing.

They take me down the stairs again, shove me into a police car, and bring me to the hospital. I give my blood sample and several hairs for another sample; the nurse is very pretty and smiling. *At least something.* Back to the police station, now they want to collect another sample – fingernails. Everything looks quite amateurish. The nail cuts are being wrapped in a simple white paper, and the police guy writes on it "right hand", "left hand". They always ask what my name is, where I live, the name of my mum… and keep writing everything down, always the same information.

It looks like it's getting dark outside, and I still don't know what's going on. Being tired is a blessing, otherwise I would probably get crazy or anxious. Tiredness somehow smooths the rough edges of what by all means seems to be a pretty shitty situation.

They take me to another room. Here are the two criminal police guys that I already know well, joined by two other people that I see for the first time. One introduces herself as a translator, the other as a state prosecutor. They start talking and right away say that I am suspected of Michael's murder.

What the hell, are they serious?! Apparently yes.

I refuse to take part in any further conversation until the Czech consul joins us. One of them walks out of the room and after a couple of minutes brings the consul in. She takes over the translation and promises to arrange a lawyer. She also recommends not answering any more questions without my legal representative. I agree. She leaves again, and the translator tries to translate the text of the accusation. She seems to be quite nice, but her translation is not great. I tell her to stop and refuse to sign anything. She seems more nervous than me at this point.

Now they leave me alone with the two police guys. I ask if I can write down a few important phone numbers from my cell phone. They agree. I use the opportunity to divert all the incoming calls to my sales manager back in Prague. He will certainly be a *little* surprised when he finds out why. One more thing – a quick text message to Jarka, my love. The last message for a long time…

The day is being wrapped up by another overnighter at the police station. *Is it normal? Are they allowed to do that to us?* I don't know but any protest seems futile. Let's sue them later. *If we get out of this shit.* Here is Ivo; we are back together again. Unfortunately, we can't talk but we look at each other and shake our heads – it is clear he was accused too. Good night!

Split, Criminal Police Station of Dalmatia 13th of September 2002

Wake up! The policeman wakes Ivo and I again, after another sleepless night on the floor. It's Friday the 13th. *I haven't brushed my teeth for three days. Shower... I don't even think about it. I am very hungry and realize that I don't even remember what my last meal was.* They take Ivo away and I am waiting. What a mess.

My 'friend' criminalist – he seems to be a deputy head of Split criminal police or something like that – comes inside and threatens me again. *An idiot. Maybe it's their tactic to weaken me so that I crack under pressure? Well, I know that I haven't done anything, so their tactics won't work.*

Why are we suspects? What nonsense! It dawns on me that they probably need to find someone guilty because one of their divers died as well. To deflect attention from the fact that he should not have been diving. His commander should not have instructed him to go into the cave. *We told them it's dangerous! Stupid, macho men.*

And the story with the knife? I don't believe it, but I also can't imagine that the Croatian rescue team – who for sure arrived after we had left – found the bodies, arranged everything, and stuck a knife into Michael's body so that they could accuse some of us. *I mean, nothing is impossible in this country but THAT would be definitely too much. Suicide?* This thought crosses my mind. *When was Michael running out of air and panicked? What would I do? Kill myself with my own scuba diving knife? Maybe, but this sounds crazy too.*

My lawyer arrives together with the consul Vera, and we are introduced to each other. He seems reasonable. He explains my options and recommends that I stop talking to the police and only provide further testimony in front of a court. Sounds good. He leaves again, and Vera too.

A couple of police guys enter the room again. I am alone with them and now they all threaten me.

"How did you do it?"

Now I lose it. I hear myself shouting as loud as I can, "Look at my fucking dive computer and see that I haven't done anything!!!" They seem to be happy that I lost my temper, for the first time, and leave again.

Are you stupid? Does it help to shout at the police?

Well, probably not, but for some reason I feel good about it. Waiting again.

After some time, which somehow feels like it is flowing around me, they pick me up and take me to the police gym. Here are all my scuba friends again! It seems like an eternity since we saw each other. They all look terrible, tired, and dirty: probably very similar to my appearance. We look at each other, just shaking our heads in disbelief. Talking is forbidden.

The gym floor is covered by our diving gear and personal belongings. Vera arrives and brings some food. Finally!!! We are told that each of us should find and collect our own stuff. Immediately, absolute chaos starts. There are several policemen in the room, and they all keep shouting conflicting instructions. *Catch-22* crosses my mind, and I can't stop smiling, which seems highly inappropriate to the situation. *WTF.*

All of us are going through the piles of gear, collecting our own, and the police officers are writing down everything. My Aladin dive computer is missing, I tell the policeman, and he claims that they have it for the investigation.

Really? What if they lose it? What if they 'lose' it intentionally? I was not diving that night; the computer records clearly show that. Are they trying to hide one of the key pieces of evidence? Bastards!

In my other bag I find Ivo's pocketknife, open. One of the policemen writes down my find in his papers. Another find is an unpacked surgical glove, one of those that I use for diving in cold water but haven't used on this trip. *Unpacked! Bloody hell, they are really trying to frame us.* Another entry into the police documents.

Ivo and I must undress and change into other clothes. Our friends are told to give us some of theirs. I got underwear and a T-shirt from Tom, shorts from Pike, and sandals from Zack. They smell like the decaying body of some animal. Yuck. Before they pack all mine and Ivo's belongings into plastic bags, I manage to steal two packs of chewing gum. At least this is something when we are still not allowed to brush our teeth. I feel that the only 'evidence' the police might have is the lie detector test. *When they first threatened me and then asked questions. Was it legal?* I only find out much later that Ivo's test was done in exactly the same way. I am being taken back to the interrogation room for some more waiting.

It's clear that we are in a pretty serious mess. I still trust that the truth will be revealed soon. *If there is some kind of god (or gods?).* I don't believe there is, but if yes – *what is he or she doing? Watching?* Interestingly enough, I feel somewhat peaceful, a strange calmness arrives to my entire body. *Well, maybe that's a good sign.* I recall what I heard on one of the recent leadership training sessions at work:

"Very often, you can't influence what happens to you in life. What happens to you is a 'result'. If you like or hate the result – it does not matter. The result does not care. If you are sad or happy or angry – it does not matter, the result is still the same. We often cannot influence what happens, but can manage our reactions, our thoughts, and sometimes what we will do about the result or the situation."

Still, my eyes fill with tears when I think about *my darling back home. And my parents! Especially my dad, he is more sensitive than my mum. Hopefully they will somehow handle the whole thing well. And… it's not over yet; this is just the beginning. How is it going to end? Our lovely scuba and sailing trip took an unexpected turn, that's for sure. Two people are dead. What a tragedy, regardless of me and Ivo being falsely accused. What about Michael's mum? He is their only child. Was. Has anyone told his family?*

The arrival of a fat policeman in uniform interrupts my reflections. He tells me to put my hands behind my back. It's here! Another movie-like situation that I have never expected to experience myself. Here come the handcuffs. Ivo walks in front of me, escorted by another policeman. They take us out of the building. A very stupid idea crosses my mind: *Now they are going to kill us, to avenge the death of their comrade.* I brush it off. We are at the court building, waiting at the calm, empty hall with tall windows and a very high ceiling.

Handcuffs are very annoying, mainly because they are behind my back. Ivo has his arms handcuffed too but in the front. *So unfair! Maybe I am the main suspect…* I ask my police guy to change them, and he refuses. OK, I must come up with a trick.

"Can I go to the bathroom, please?"

My escort shakes his head but moves the cuffs to the front. The first little success! Hopefully there is more to come.

Now our Vera joins us, it feels like we have known each other for ages. She talks to Ivo first, then me. She is so nice, but is looking tired too. It must be difficult for her as well. She says that everything will be all right (really?) and that she will talk to the judge. Our lawyers arrive. Mine is well dressed in a nice suit and serious tie. Ivo's lawyer is a woman in her forties, and she makes a good impression. While she and Ivo are in the courtroom, I am able to tell my lawyer the whole story. Luckily we can communicate in English as my Croatian is far from perfect. Yet.

Now it's our turn. I am a bit nervous but tell myself to calm down. *We haven't done anything!* The judge looks like a judge, serious but seems intelligent and neutral – unlike the criminal police folks. I have a chance to explain what happened. The state prosecutor asks several questions. One question really brings a shock: "Where is your dive computer?" *Bastards!* My answer is that the criminal police in the gym confirmed that they have it for the investigation. Otherwise, everything seems all right. *Are they letting us go?*

There is a short break. My lawyer talks to the police guys and the judge. It's a small town, and they all seem to know each other well. During the break, Ivo and I have a first brief chance to exchange a couple of words. "*Komplot*," he says, speaking Czech.

"Yes, they are trying to frame us." I nod. "This is pretty messed up."

Ivo continues. "Last night, five policemen had me alone in the room and they threatened me! They said that they will beat me if I don't confess that I murdered Michael. Later they changed tack and said that I can be free the next day if I testify that you did it."

Motherfuckers! OK, it seems that the battle has begun. Battle for nothing that important in the grand scheme of the universe. 'Just' for our freedom.

The judge invites us back to the courtroom and orders one month of custody jail to provide more time for further police investigation. Then everything goes very fast: the policemen take us to the car and drive across the town at an incredible speed. Ivo has handcuffs and I don't. They forgot!

"We have tons of time," I say to the speeding police driver, testing my rough Croatian. They both start laughing but keep the speed.

He turns his head around, and I wish he would keep his eyes on the road. "My duty finishes at eleven, my nervous wife expects me at home. No time to waste!"

Ivo and I can't stop laughing too, what a conversation. It would be really funny if we were not on the way to a custody prison.

We stop with screeching tires in front of the building which certainly looks like a jail. White building. Windows with bars. Steel gate. Barbed wire. We have no idea for how long it will be our 'home'.

Our policemen hand us over to the guards and leave. We are standing while waiting in the corridor.

"Follow me," says one of the guards, and we enter a small room.

"Everything out of your pockets."

We are starting to understand the Croatian language more and more. My belongings are not that impressive: clothes from scuba friends, the passport, and one pack of chewing gums – the other was a precious gift to Ivo.

They tell me to undress and one of the guards puts on a rubber glove. *Another movie scene! Bloody hell.* But luckily, they only look at us and one searches through our stuff using the gloved hand. What a relief!

From my amazing property I can keep everything except for the passport, chewing gum, and the string from my shorts. Pike will be disappointed that he lost his string but hopefully he will accept the reasons and inevitability of such loss. I go out, Ivo in. He wears Michael's T-shirt and sandals. What irony. I wonder, *When will we see each other again?*

They give me a blanket, a pillow, two bedsheets, and a metal mug. *Yay, I will sleep with a blanket and hopefully in a bed too, after three nights on the floor!* Here comes my cell. No. 25. *Three guys here, is it appropriate to call them 'mates' in this scenario?* We shake hands, a wonderful Slavic custom in any situation, and introduce each other. They show me my bed, an upper bunk on the left side of the room. I make my bed, the mug goes to the small cabinet next to it, have a quick chat with the 'mates' and say good night. *Finally, a proper bed!*

I am so tired but obviously can't just fall asleep right away.

This is quite incredible. I am in jail! Who would have thought so just one week ago? Am I scared? Probably too tired to feel any strong emotions now. Has anyone told my family and Jarka? What do lawyers think, do they consider us innocent or have doubts? Too many questions…

Finally, a quiet, warm Mediterranean night calms me down and I fall into a sleep without dreams. One last thought crosses my mind before drifting away: *First night behind the bars in my life! What an experience! How many more?*

Split, Zatvor Bilica, Dan's cell
14th of September 2002

I am in jail. The words forming this sentence are quite spectacular and rather unexpected. My roommates are all locals: Dragan, drug dealer, speaks English; Vladimir, drug dealer, speaks little English; and finally Goran, killed his wife, speaks German. Lovely team. I don't know it yet, but our room will be called by all actors here, prisoners and guards alike, 'Two dealers, two killers'.

I was a little afraid of what to expect from our collective. It's my first time in jail after all. Nevertheless, everyone seems to be pretty cool and calm. Let's see.

The room is a rectangular space; we've got a television, newspapers are delivered every day, and there is an Asian-style toilet with a sink in one of the corners behind a small wall. We also have a fan, a small window to the west (barred, of course), and a dining table with a plastic tablecloth decorated by green and red apples. We've got everything we need!

The jail routine is rather straightforward:

6:30	Wake up by the lights on
7:00	Breakfast that usually consists of white bread with butter and jam
7:30	Medicines supply for those who need it + delivery of the newspaper
8:00	Usually another round of sleep, either until lunch or until the 'fresh-air walk' (*boravak na svježem zraku*). The walk lasts for two hours, we join some other rooms
12:00	Lunch
13:00	Yet another round of sleep, watching tv, reading books
18:00	Dinner
18:30	Another round of tv
23:00	Lights out, but one can watch tv all night long

Simply said: food and sleep. *What else can a man wish for?*

Oh, I nearly forgot – there is a room check by the guards three times a day. Most of thc time this consists of a few bangs on the window bars by the baton. *Not very thorough*, I think, already planning my escape…

Two times a week we go to the showers and in between there are visits of lawyers or relatives, and on and on, always the same. If you have money on a special 'jail account', you can visit a small shop two times a week and buy cigarettes, snacks, and some basic toiletries.

Boys usually speak in Croatian; I understand but of course not everything. I wonder for how long I will have to be here to learn the language well. They are quite curious as to why I am so calm.

"I haven't done anything."

They just laugh. "That's what we all say here."

The only things that really suck, besides the pure fact of being in jail, is that I haven't had a shower for four days, and I haven't brushed my teeth for four days. No one from our civilized society in the developed world can imagine how bad it feels not to be able to brush teeth. *Could one get used to it?* Anyway, it sucks. Moreover, there seems to be no light at the end of the tunnel, as I don't have a brush, neither toothpaste nor soap. Also, no money, at least not yet. The boys are great; they lend me a piece of soap so that I can at least wash a bit in the sink.

Food is much better than expected, so at least that's something. Would be interesting to compare it with the jail food in Czech. Well, maybe there will be a chance…

Newspapers arrive. Newspapers in jail, that's unexpected! *Slobodna Dalmacija*. The front page shows our sailing boat and the story shouts that we killed Michael. Of course, it also covers how a heroic Croatian diver perished in the rescue operation. My full name as well as Ivo's are included. *Fuck. Fucking police bastards.* They leaked our names to the press so that the entire country now hates us.

During the walk, other prisoners keep asking questions, and everyone knows by now who I am and what I 'did'. The best tactic to avoid discussions seems to be to pretend that I don't understand.

Evening TV news is here. Not surprisingly, we are one of the headline stories. I am very, very scared now. My job back home is full of marketing, PR, and media.

I know very well how powerful they are. Regardless of whether they write the truth or not. Now everyone 'knows', at least in Croatia for sure. What about back home?

Is it possible that their plot is going to work? That they will be able to manufacture enough evidence to sentence Ivo and me? Or the judge will simply collaborate with the police and play the game? Shit.

I can't stop tears from running down my cheeks. *My love, where are you and do you know by now?*

Prague, Unilever Corporate Headquarters
Still the same day, 14th of September 2002

"Hey Jarka, a phone call for you! From Croatia," says the voice in the headset, and Jarka tells them to transfer it. She has been working for Unilever for a couple of years now, first in Slovakia, then she moved to Prague. That's where she met her new love, Dan. He is a member of the board here, but Jarka doesn't care, these things don't mean a lot to her. She simply loves him and can't wait for him to come back from the sailing trip to Croatia.

I must admit (to myself only, I would never reveal it to anyone else) that I really miss him and that I am quite nervous too because he usually texts me every day. Just a short message but we both know that we are here for each other. He has not texted for two days now!

The call comes in: "Jarka here, hello?"

"Hello, are you the girlfriend of Daniel Frolec?" says the voice from the headset, in a rather official tone.

"Hmmm… yes… why are you asking? Who are you?"

"My name is Vera. I am Czech consul in Croatia. Your partner was arrested here in Split and is a suspect in a murder case. I understand such news might be difficult for you. I am sorry. Nevertheless, could you inform his parents and the employer, please?"

Jarka feels drops of cold sweat running down her spine, and her hand grips the phone headset even tighter.

"Oh… yes… I guess… I could do that. Could you tell me more, what happened?"

Vera seems to be friendly but is clearly busy too. "I have to handle a couple urgent matters now, but here is my number, please call me later this afternoon and we can talk more."

"Thank you, yes, I will call you for sure!"

What? My mind starts racing. What nonsense! He definitely did not kill anyone. But the whole thing seems real. What a nightmare.

Jarka is not sure what to do first, but somewhat her mind clears up and like in a dream she watches herself standing up and walking into the office of her boss, one of the other company board members, to tell him what happened. A couple of minutes later both of them are knocking on the door of the company chairwoman's office.

Her assistant opens the door and invites them in. The chairwoman is just talking to her other assistant, explaining something while pointing at the computer monitor. After finishing her sentence, she turns towards us: "Oh, what brings you here all of a sudden? You seem quite upset, Jarka? Unfortunately, my day is chock-a-block, full of meetings."

Jarka explains what she knows, which is not much but nevertheless quite a bombshell. The chairwoman, a measured lady in her fifties, seems to be calm and relaxed. Surprised, of course, but still calm.

"Lada, please cancel all my meetings for the rest of the day." She jumps into action immediately, talking to one of her personal assistants. "Organize an emergency board meeting in one hour. Whoever can make it should attend. Oh, ask our PR director to join us too, we might need him."

She turns towards Jarka, lightly touching her shoulder. "Let's all meet in the boardroom in an hour. Don't worry, everything will be fine, Jarka. Dan in jail? This must be some kind of misunderstanding."

I am not sure about that, but having supportive people around me for sure helps.

Most of the board members are able to assemble despite such short notice. Everyone is of course curious to hear why there is such an emergency meeting. Very unusual for a large company like ours. Jarka knows all the faces, including the PR director who joined us too. They are all men, except for the chairwoman, of course. They look a bit surprised, wondering what the reason might be that Jarka, one of the board members' assistants, sits in one of the chairs around the large board table.

The chairwoman takes the lead: "Thank you for coming. I understand that it's not always easy to meet so fast. Let's make it short, effective, and factual. We are here because one of our dear colleagues, Dan, is in trouble. Jarka, would you explain what you know now, please."

"Yes, thank you all for coming, indeed. I really appreciate it. As most of you probably know, Dan and I are… hmmm… partners. I just received a call from Croatia, from the Czech consulate. Dan was accused of murder."

That's what she manages to say quite clearly, but then her voice betrays her, her eyes filling up with tears.

After a brief moment of complete silence, everyone starts to speak at the same time.

"Dan accused of murder? Impossible."

"Unbelievable."

"Do you know more?"

Many voices are coming from all directions at the same time.

"Hey, hey, calm down, gents." The Chairwoman breaks into the conundrum. "Of course, this is rather unexpected and perhaps even crazy but let's give Jarka a chance to explain more."

Meanwhile, Jarka is able to regain composure: "Well, it's not every day that I receive such phone calls…"

Everyone starts laughing despite how serious the whole situation seems to be. Jarka carries on explaining what the consul told her and about the holiday trip, sailing boat, and scuba diving with friends.

"That's all I know now," she concludes.

"All right, guys, let's see what we can do," the chairwoman says.

Jarka thinks to herself: *I never really liked her too much but the way she handles the meeting and all the testosterone around the room is for sure impressive.*

"Dan remains a suspect. He is innocent until proven guilty. That's what we will respect for sure. Jarka will get all our help, moral, financial, whatever is required." She turns towards Jarka. "Just ask, please. Anything. For the rest, no one is allowed to talk to the press except for myself and Richard, our PR director, that's why I called him into the meeting. Richard, any ideas, any recommendations?"

Richard is a serious guy in his forties, good-looking perhaps, aside from a little bit of belly fat slightly visible under his suit. Quite a weird thought crosses Jarka's mind given the circumstances: *He should stop eating all those typical Czech meals.*

"Thank you all for coming," says Richard. "Indeed, innocent until proven otherwise. This will be our storyline if the press asks and trust me, they will. I will draft a press release describing Dan as one of our top leaders, always reliable with high personal integrity. Innocent until proven guilty and so on. You will have the press release in your inbox within the next hour. Any questions from the nosy journalists – just send them to me and I will deal with it. Oh, and one more thing. Jarka, you will be hunted, and we can't stop that. What we could do though, give you a crash course PR training today or tomorrow morning. Let's discuss it after this meeting."

Everyone nods. Everything makes sense. Jarka still seems worried but at the same time impressed as to how these businesspeople can handle such crazy situations. She feels delighted by all the support. The chairwoman concludes the meeting, and she hugs her – *what an unexpected move!* – before leaving the boardroom, then all the board members stand up, some hug Jarka too and others shake her hand. *What a day!*

It's not over yet, she discovers back in her office. *Now I must talk to Dan's parents! We have been on and off together for a year now, but I haven't met them yet! I hope they at least know that I exist… Let's get on with it.*

One hour later, Jarka finds herself in front of their apartment in the Prague suburbs.

Ring, ring.

The doorbell sound rings inside the flat. After a while the door opens and there stands Dan's mum, still a good-looking and fit woman in her fifties.

"Yes… hello… uhm… how can I help you, miss?"

"I am Jarka, Dan's girlfriend. Can I come in, please?"

"Of course." Dan's mum invites her inside. Jarka takes off her shoes in the narrow hall and is being led into a living room. *How can they fit all this antique furniture here, into a living room of a typical small flat?* Dan's dad sits in an armchair, watching television. He comes across as a kind, gentle man, still with good hair, some of them starting to grey on the sides.

Now he stands up and shakes Jarka's hand with a question mark in his eyes. "Please, take a seat, nice to meet you. Dan told us about you. Yes, he did. But we were wondering when or if he will introduce us."

"Nice of him that he mentioned me. You might be wondering what's the reason for this unannounced visit. I came to tell you something…" Jarka is going to explain but her shaking voice is interrupted by the jingle of the main evening news. *I hate TVs! Haven't had one for at least ten years now.*

"Let me switch off the sound here." Dan's dad reaches for the remote control to reduce the volume, but he freezes before he's able to finish his move. His son, well, a picture of his son, wearing a blue T-shirt, stares from the television screen.

The news host exclaims in a rather excited tone of voice that "Two Czech divers were accused of murder in Croatia and are now being held in custody in Split."

Jarka and Dan's parents look at each other, everyone clearly shocked.

The host continues to explain: "One of the divers from the group was found dead in an underwater cave with his diving knife in the chest. The chief of Dalmatian regional police has not yet released more details, citing sensitivity of the investigation as one of the Croatian Navy divers got lost and died in the cave during the rescue operation on the following day. We will report more on this case as soon as we know more, our correspondent is already on the way to Split. Now, let's move to the imminent danger of floods in Northern Bohemia…"

Dan's dad finally manages to turn the sound off. They all look at each other, an awkward moment of silence. No one knows what to say.

"Yes, that's why I am here. Czech consul in Croatia called me a couple hours ago, asked me to inform the company and of course you too. I am sorry, what news, oh my god." Jarka's voice trails away and her eyes glisten with suppressed tears.

"Oh, I don't know what to think about it," says Mum slowly. "I don't believe any of this, obviously, Dan is not a murderer."

"Sure, this can't be true, my dear." Dad shakes his head. "But what are we going to do? Imagine, our Danik is now in jail!" He exhales deeply.

Mum turns towards Jarka. "Thank you very much for coming to inform us. I know it must be very hard for you too. For all of us. What else do you know, please? Oh, do you like to have a cup of tea or a glass of water, I forgot to ask you. We don't drink coffee, so I can't offer."

Jarka asks for a glass of water and continues to explain little pieces of information she got from the consul. "She promised to call me back later today and tell me more."

And that's how Jarka met Dan's parents. One can hardly imagine a more improbable situation of meeting the future in-laws.

Split, Zatvor Bilica, Dan's cell
15th of September 2002

Today is a big day! After being so tired and so devastated and so desperate last night, I woke up to a completely different reality. *Crazy how our minds (or at least mine...) work!* I am fresh, full of energy, and in my typical way – *Jarka hates my positive-thinking thing; let's see how useful it will be here* – I start making plans for today:

1. Design a daily fitness routine to stay sane.

2. Make sure to stop worrying, TRUST that the truth will be revealed.

3. Write down the whole story, reconstruct a timeline of the events.

4. Summarize arguments, reasons why neither Ivo nor me could have killed Michael.

Let's start right away. Good news: I seem to have tons of available time!

So, the daily fitness will be: 3x10 push-ups for biceps and triceps, 3x10 push-ups for chest and shoulders, 3x30 squats and 3x15 abdominal curls. Done. Every day.

How to stay calm and trust the universe? I have no idea how to do that but somehow feel that breathing can help. Every day, do at least ten minutes of breathing exercises: one set for the diaphragm elasticity and the other to simply relax. Once in the morning, once before the lights go off. Done.

The third list item will of course take some time – let's not forget that I have plenty of that – but I decide to start right away. Luckily, I have several sheets of white A4 paper from my lawyer. *Dammit! No pencil.* I have never thought about how priceless a pencil could be. I summon some courage and ask one of the roommates. He gives me a pencil without any questions! *Here we go, the luck is back,* I catch myself thinking, what a silly conclusion after such a trivial success. Nevertheless, I can start.

How was it in all the crime novels that I read during my teenage years? Motif, opportunity, weapon, witnesses, cause of death, marks, or points of evidence… let's create a mind map, the kind of spider drawing that one of my work colleagues taught me a few years ago. I owe him a pint. Or two. Quite handy – he probably did not envisage its usage in my present circumstances. Nor did I…

Another piece must be a timeline, what happened when and who was there. As detailed as possible while my short-term memory still has everything stored properly inside of the brain.

Oh yes, and any open questions, anything that must be found out, any arguments for and against our involvement in the events of that night.

Everything is coming together well, and everything makes sense! Or at least that's what I think. This activity dramatically improves my mood and at the same time helps me trust that everything will be fine.

Well done, Dan! The lawyer will roll his eyes when he sees the product of my work.

Split, Zatvor Bilica, Dan's cell 16th of September 2002

Today is another 'great' day.

The morning newspaper arrived, and the image of our sailing boat is on the front page again. The article builds on a previous story and sensationally uncovers the murder motive: a row among homosexuals on board. Michael became jealous about Dan and Ivo being together, a brawl ensued, Michael was murdered and thrown into the cave.

I can't believe what I read, what a next-level mess.

The truth indeed does not matter here. No one cares that none of us is gay. Police will simply come up with anything that suits them and moreover they will share everything with the media. Being labelled as gay while at the same time being in prison does not look like a good combination, I feel.

Fuck.

On top of that, the text celebrates Olan, the navy diver who died in the rescue mission, depicting him as a true hero.

Fuck times two.

A Croatian soldier died because of the Czech gays killing each other. Unbelievable but quite dangerous. Most of the people who read the newspaper will think that that's exactly what happened. We are stuffed.

My roommates read the article, giggle a bit, but make no remarks or anything against me. For now, at least.

One of the guards opens the door and we go for a walk which means two hours is spent outdoors, in the square inner courtyard of the prison building. High walls all around but one can at least see the sky. There are around a dozen inhabitants from the other rooms. People sit, some walk around the perimeter, some exercise, others play football. I normally enjoy this daily dose of fresh air but today, after the newspaper news, I feel somewhat apprehensive. I am sure all the other guys read the article.

How will they react to the 'information' that I am supposedly gay?

Before there is a chance to find out, the guard calls my name and escorts me out of the courtyard. My lawyer is here. I try to explain that there are some important notes in my room that I need for the meeting, but he does not care and takes me straight to the visitor's room. *Without my precious notes!* I feel desperate.

The lawyer has lots of *'good news'*: he has not seen my dive computer yet and apparently they found blood on the boat. *Bloody hell!* I am trying to think… "Oh yes, there was the paint from the mooring which stained the bow at the Maslenica harbour!"

So, either there are some stains which the police consider to be blood, and they will find out it's not blood. Alternatively, as I don't trust anyone here, police guys already found out it's not blood, but they added some to make sure we are stuffed. Balkan! Let's see.

"How much time do you have?" I ask the lawyer. "Perhaps I will be able to recall everything that I wrote down yesterday."

"I've got five more minutes before I must leave and visit the court." He shows me his calendar with other cases. *Now, that's really comforting!*

"Do you trust that we, Ivo and I, are innocent?" is my last question.

"I don't know," he says. He stands up, we shake hands, and the door closes behind him.

I feel like I am on a roller-coaster. One moment I am happy and convinced everything will be all right. Next, my mood sharply deteriorates and a feeling of desperation creeps in.

What if they manage to frame us here? How many years in prison?

Wow.

The guard takes me to the prison psychologist. *What?* I am surprised they have anything like that here. Nevertheless, the guy seems to need a therapist himself, nothing impressive.

If you can be so arrogant, I tell myself, *either it's not so bad with you yet or you are really angry and try to take it out on others. Stop it!* continues the talk in my head. *Let's not get crazy about one stupid lawyer, even though my life perhaps depends on him and his ability to understand the situation, what happened, what did not happen, and his ability to convince others about it. But if he does not trust that we are innocent, how effectively can he defend me?*

The psychologist asks me if I have any issues. "Ha ha, no, I am absolutely fine, on holidays in sunny Cambodia, oh sorry, Croatia!" He talks and moves very, very slowly, probably to save energy in the summer heat. In any case, he is sweating profoundly. I collect myself, use the opportunity to tell him that I don't have anything. He is quite nice. He gives me a toothbrush (!), toothpaste, soap, toilet paper, and hair shampoo. *What a catch!*

Otherwise, *the day is pretty shitty,* I must admit. Few swear words in Croatian that I already learned are very useful now. On the other hand, no one can imagine how amazing it feels to brush your teeth for the first time in six days!

Our room has a canteen visit today but I don't have any money. At least I can have a look at what they sell and walk around the building, accompanied by my roommates and a couple of guards, of course. One of them gives me a document with the indictment and announcement of the custody.

Brilliant.

Split, Zatvor Bilica, Ivo's cell still 16th of September 2002

Ivo sits on his bed. A bunk in the jail, to be precise. Many thoughts run through his head.

I am suspected of murder or at least of assistance in such a crime. What a crazy turn of events. It looked like such a great idea to join Dan on this trip. I trusted that we would have a good time sailing, and now this. Unexpected, to say the least.

Ivo is not sure what to think about the whole situation. He contemplates different options. *Of course, no one from the boat had any chance to commit the crime that the police came up with. Their hypothesis is completely stupid. Even though… Dan could have done it but there was no reason. No, he absolutely didn't do it, I know him too well. Michael got lost in the cave, that's for sure. I saw him leaving alone from the boat to join the other guys. But what about the knife? Could anyone kill themselves while lost in an underwater cave, running out of air? Weird but not impossible. Alternatively, the specialist rescue team planted the knife into his dead body after they found him, just to make sure someone could be accused. Possible, but highly unlikely.*

Earlier, still at the police station, it was a shit show. Police tried to frame Dan and Ivo by threatening them, putting them through the lie detector and during the interrogation surprising them with suggestive questions. *Is this how such lie detector procedure should be?* Ivo is not certain, yet he feels that in Croatia *anything is possible.*

On top of everything, the navy diver is dead too. Such a wasteful death. Tom clearly told them not to dive there without proper gear and training. Well, in any case, this holiday took a very interesting twist.

Ivo's mood changes from sad to anxious, and the talk in his head continues. *What if they succeed in framing us here? I am not angry at anyone, but I feel like I'm in a judicial error movie where innocent people get sentenced for 20 years in jail. Could this happen to me? It looks like it can. The maximum sentence for murder in Croatia is 40 years… I will have to come up with some ideas on what to do with my life.*

For now, let's focus on the present moment, he tells himself.

When he looks around, the picture seems rather bleak. A small cell with five other guys. Six bunkbeds, a table with two benches, TV set. Yes, there is a TV in the jail here! Not just local TV channels; they are showing an American movie with local subtitles! A standing-style toilet with a sink in the corner. Everyone has a little bedside table. Ivo's is empty.

How is Dan doing? He is likely in a similar room, somewhere in this building. Ivo does not feel angry. *Dan has always been a good friend and is in the same situation now, against his will. Hopefully we will manage to get out of this shit.* Ivo somehow trusts the universe that the truth will be revealed. *But when?* This is not clear at all, especially looking at the local newspaper with the story on the front page, with full names, describing how a bunch of homosexuals holidaying in Croatia killed his 'friend' and threw him in a cave.

What chaos.

His roommates look at the newspaper and start talking fast to each other. Ivo doesn't understand everything.

"Guys, what are you talking about?"

"What?" replies one of them, a guy with a bald head, a tattoo of a snake on his forearm.

"I say, what you talk about?" Ivo tries with simplified English, trying to explain what he meant.

"They say you gay. Not good in Croatia," says the other mate, tall, skinny, with most of his hair grey despite being in his forties. The other prisoners just look at each other, clearly understanding what's being discussed but don't speak any English.

"No, me not gay," replies Ivo rather impatiently. "Why not good in Croatia?"

Snake Tattoo tries to answer: "In here, lot of people go church. Church say 'not good homosexual'. People believe."

"I have a wife at home. No gay."

The guys look at each other, talk in their language. Ivo does not get everything but understands that they are discussing his sexual preferences.

"We trust," skinny guy explains. "But local people, police, the judge don't know. Difficult for you."

"*Hvala*," answers Ivo. He has already learned a few words and this one means 'thank you', but he is not sure what it means for him. He is not gay but now the whole country has read the news, so everyone considers him to be homosexual. What does it mean for the case? Who knows.

A different idea crosses his mind: *I have always enjoyed learning new languages, perhaps there is an opportunity to learn one that I have never thought about. Actually, that's a great idea! If I manage to learn Croatian, I will be able to understand the judge, lawyers, my roommates. Let's start right now. What's the movie about?*

Split, Zatvor Bilica, Dan's cell 17th of September 2002

Tuesday, the day of relatives' visits. I am curious if anyone will arrive while not really counting on it. The distance between Prague and Split is more than 1,000 kilometres, quite a drive. *What does such a visit look like?* Lawyer meetings seem to be done in a simple, boring room sitting around a table. With the guards outside, of course. I wonder, *Are private visits the same? What if my fox comes here?! Is it possible to hug each other?* Such a vision brings tears to my eyes, so I better kick it out of my mind so as not to be disappointed later.

What if she does not arrive? What if no one visits me? What if Jarka won't be allowed to come to the prison? If police keep this stupid idea about the homosexual motive, she might have to be one of the witnesses. I am so scared! My usual tendency is to think about me first. Not anymore! I realize that for the first time in my life I care much more about someone else. Such a beautiful feeling. *Did I need a prison experience to find out? I am very worried about her. If she is the only one that can dismiss the allegations about my homosexuality, what if something happens to her? What if the navy colleagues of the deceased diver find out? What if they kill her to avoid her testimony? Anything is possible in this country. I feel like I'm in a movie again. But it's my life!* Perhaps I am getting paranoid, but I can't help feeling serious anxiety. Not about myself at all, but about my love.

I must convince her not to come!

The visit is here! I see myself as if I was outside of my body and in some kind of trance, walking with five other prisoners. Only one of them is from my room. I don't know the others. Ivo is nowhere to be seen. We arrive in a larger room divided by cross bars with glass in between. Five chairs on one side of the glass, five on the other. Like in the movies indeed!

On the other side, I see Vera from the Czech consulate and… my love, Jarka, is here too!!! *She looks so beautiful.* I sit down facing her, the glass dividing us. There is something like a grille with holes so that we can talk. But I can't! My eyes fill with tears. I press my hand against glass and her hand meets mine from the other side. The footsteps of a guard behind me disturb this emotional moment. My feelings are confusing: simultaneously I feel very happy to see her while at the same time devasted that there is bullet-proof glass separating us. I am a little proud and relieved too – *she really came to see me!* My original plan for the visit was to be calm, no complaints, no bad news, so that she does not get frightened. The plan did not work out. We look at each other and start talking at last, both at the same time.

"I love you," Jarka says.

"I love you too."

"It's absurd. Of course, I trust that you haven't done anything. Your mum and dad are here too but the prison allowed only one person. We've got ten minutes. How are you doing?"

"I am all right. How do you feel?"

"I am OK. Your parents say hi, they love you. We brought you some clothes and books. Your friends Monika and Filip are so nice, they came with me too. How is the food here?"

"Food is no problem. The issue is that I am stuck here!"

"Everyone is trying to help, all your friends are gathering contacts to politicians, businessmen, anyone that could possibly help."

"Get me out of here! Police are fabricating evidence. Get me back to Czech."

"We will try. How is your lawyer?"

"He is not smart enough AND he doesn't trust me. I need another one, someone truly intelligent who could learn to understand scuba diving basics – the whole case is about diving physics and medicine, we could not possibly have done what we are accused of. I have thought about it for a long time. I need a lawyer who can understand it."

"OK, I will stay here and find someone."

"NO! It's dangerous for you here, you must go home! You can't walk around alone! I think that I am a little paranoid about it, but police say that we are a bunch of gays. You are clear evidence that I am not…"

Sounds of the baton hitting one of the chairs mean that our ten minutes are gone. Guards escort me and the other mates out of the room, Jarka and I are kissing each other in the air, I manage to wave my hand at the consul. That's it. Another round of mates enters the room and starts talking to their relatives on the other side. Tears, gestures, sadness, joy… everything mixed up in this one point in time and space.

I feel like *I'm at the bottom of the ocean. It's all a blur. Such strong emotions! I just want to curl up in my bed and forget about everything.* But the eventful day is not over yet. Showers are coming up!

Finally, I sigh with relief, even though an immediate thought crosses my mind: *Dark shower room, steam everywhere, prisoners all around, no guards… and I will for sure drop my soap… Are you stupid? What is this nonsense mind chatter about?*

Luckily, I've got shampoo in a sachet instead of soap, and we shower in one room at a time. Four independent showers. The place does not look fantastic, but I feel ecstatic. *I haven't had a shower for one week! So good.* I smile to myself, imagining what some of my friends with large houses and luxurious apartments would say about such a bathroom. *Hot water! What a blessing. Let's finish with a cold shower, like at home.*

The evening guard visit brings food as well as a letter from my love. What a day! Up and down. I am so happy now, falling peacefully into a good night's sleep. Shower and food, what else could one need?

Split, Zatvor Bilica, Dan's cell
18th of September 2002

Breakfast, exercise, TV, nap, rolling on the bed, lunch, more rolling on the bed, walking in the courtyard. The routine is very simple. The only 'exciting' time is the outdoor part. My roommates are OK and are used to my presence now. Not so much the other prisoners! They constantly try to ask me something or talk to one of the roommates and send him to speak to me. He looks harmless, the oldest and shortest from the whole gang. Everyone is laughing at him, probably considering him a little crazy.

Earlier in the room I was contemplating how to react to the other guys. Good question. It would be best to ignore them and only react in the case of some open provocation or aggression to show them that I am not a coward. My tactics of avoidance seem to work. They leave me alone when there is no reaction. Our room has already got the nickname *Two Dealers, Two Killers* based on the alleged crimes. Perhaps it's not worth messing with me, they think. If only they knew. I try to appear tough, ha ha, and sharp. Luckily, I can't see myself otherwise I would have to laugh.

Windows on the eastern side of the courtyard lead into an internal prison corridor. *Look who is there!* Ivo is walking in the corridor with some other mates. He stops in front of one of the windows, looks down, and our eyes meet. He raises his hand; I can't help myself and show him the OK scuba diving hand signal, thumb and index finger meeting to create an 'o'. Both of us are weirdly smiling; everything will be fine. Maybe. This was the last time we see each other in the jail.

The evening brings a huge envelope full of letters and printed emails – from my mum and dad, my love, my friends, colleagues from work… and dramatically improves my mood.

Split, Zatvor Bilica, Dan's cell
19th of September 2002

I decided to work on our case every day. Going through everything, all my notes, arguments for our innocence, adding a list of open questions, press clipping relevant articles from the Croatian newspapers. It is interesting that something new enters my mind every time I go through the material. I try to summarize the key arguments for our defence.

Also, I must find a way to memorize everything important in case the guards won't allow me to bring my notes to the meeting with the lawyer like last time. *How on earth to do that? Oh, I know! Some kind of system with symbols is needed. Let me see: list the key arguments one by one, add a number to each, come up with a symbol next to every number. Dive computer, knife, decompression sickness and so on. Bingo!* I am very happy with my work. I go through everything several times and before long I know it by heart. Now, let's have discipline to review the whole list often so I am fully prepared for the next lawyer meeting.

The afternoon sleepy atmosphere is interrupted by the canteen visit. Everyone is super excited! I mean, everyone who's got money in the prison account. It works as a deposit – someone deposits cash at the prison office, and they establish some kind of 'jail' bank account which you can spend from. The canteen visits don't happen every day as the rooms must rotate. Our room goes every Monday and Thursday.

Here we go, a small counter, basic stuff: some food, stationery, cleaning items, and more. My folks luckily deposited some money, so today I can buy this notepad, three pencils, envelopes, post stamps, shaving stuff, hair shampoo *(from a Unilever competitor, what to do!),* three packets of Marlboro cigarettes – all my mates are wondering why as I don't smoke, but I learned in Moscow during my studies that Marlboro cigarettes are always valuable currency – a large bottle of Coke, sparkling water, vitamin C, the Croatian version of Parma ham called *pršut,* and some chocolate. My heart skips a beat from all this abundance.

Coke, chocolate, *pršut* and cigarettes are not for me, they are for our room as I thought it would make sense to put together some kind of '*newbie in the room*' celebration. *Where did I get all this emotional intelligence from?* Boys are laughing, patting me on the back.

Dragan, one of the drug dealers who speaks English, explains that "a welcome party is called *ulaznica* here. How did you know it's a custom?"

"I did not know but thought that we deserve a little celebration. My girlfriend is here, you all got visitors the other day. It sucks to be here, but we should keep a positive mood, I guess."

"That's right," chimes in Vladimir, munching on the ham. "It sucks here but we should be positive. I like it."

Goran takes some chocolate and lights up a Marlboro. He only speaks German, so I ask him in Croatian, "*Kako si Goran?*" So much I have learned already. He lights up. "*Hvala ljepa,*" he says, which means 'thanks a lot'. He killed his wife. His mood seems to be usually quite dark but now he seems to be having a good time.

"So, how do you like our little *izlaznica*?" Perhaps I saw it written somewhere. The boys start immediately laughing.

"It's *ulaznica*, you silly. *Izlaznica* means 'farewell' and one must offer a roasted lamb. We are all far from a farewell party here."

I join the laugh. It feels good, this little collection of people who have at least for some time a joint destiny.

Indeed, this is not a farewell, I am thinking. *Let's see when that can be organized!*

After the feast I shave for the first time in many days. Great. I don't look like a prisoner any longer… I climb up to my bunk and start writing the journal.

Split, Zatvor Bilica, Dan's cell
20th of September 2002

Friday. Tonight, I will have been behind bars for one week. *Not bad,* I am thinking, *after the first day of desperation (I was so tired! And without teeth brushing, remember) I feel all right.* Sometimes it seems like we are in some kind of scout camp or a hospital. If only there was not a piece of paper with a murder charge in my cupboard…

Lawyer nowhere. Good mood switches to bad, peace changes into stress. Back and forth. More peace. Nevertheless… I am still very worried about my fox. *What if something happens to her?* I would give anything to know that she is all right. It's weird how we got used to instantly communicating with each other and now this feature of life is completely missing. When I feel that bad mood or perhaps depression is coming, I manage to identify it and force my mind to move somewhere else. Often with success; it's funny how it works.

We can manage our minds!

Sometimes it takes more effort, and I must start doing something: exercise, writing, or breathing.

The prison is for sure good in some aspects. For example, fitness – I exercise every day, sometimes twice. *I must remember this and carry on after they let me go!* Hopefully they will, of course.

The guard opens the door at an unusual time and gives me a document. Power of attorney for a new lawyer!!! Signed by my love. *Wow, so she has managed to find someone else. Let's see…* I am very happy, even though I don't remember the lawyer's name. The newspaper reports that all the members of our scuba group testified in front of the judge and said that Ivo and I are innocent. *At least something positive.*

Another round of showers today, my second in the jail. The routine starts to be clear and somewhat comforting too.

Split Harbour, Sailboat *Domani*
20th of September 2002

The sailing boat is gently moving from side to side, tied up to the moorings in the harbour surrounded by beautiful mediaeval buildings. The whole scene would look so peaceful if it were not for what's happening inside of the boat's crammed salon.

"What the fuck," says Zack, "they keep interrogating us, took away our passports, I must go back to Prague – my boss is getting nervous and my wife and kids... Let's not even talk about it."

"Yes, stupid police came up with a crime which had never happened and now we are stuck here," joins in Roman, clearly getting nervous.

Tom feels like he must jump in. "Hey, let's keep it down, boys," he says in a raised voice. "No one could expect to go home when there are two dead bodies lying in the mortuary."

"Yes, that's clear," confirms Pike in his usually calm voice. "Nevertheless, don't worry, guys, they will have to let us go soon, now that they arrested Dan and Ivo."

"But what about them?" asks Pete. "Are we going to leave them behind? They obviously haven't done anything!"

The atmosphere on board is getting tense. No one believes that Dan and Ivo committed any crime, it was clearly impossible, but everyone is anxious to have this 'holiday' behind them.

"Let's have one minute silence for our friend and the dead diver too, folks," Zack says and everyone nods, grateful for this change of mood.

"Let's also think about our two buddies that are somewhere in the jail now and wish for them to be released soon," adds Tom.

The whole crew stops talking and immerses themselves in the silence. The atmosphere changes and becomes calm, even positive one could say. The ocean outside is calm too, gently rocking the boat from one side to the other.

Split, Zatvor Bilica, Dan's cell
21st of September 2002

Finally! The weekend is here! We don't have to do anything or go anywhere... oops, we can't go anywhere anyway!

My sister has her birthday, at least that's what I reckon. Can't call her so it doesn't matter anyway. My roommates are still very good. I think that I was very lucky with this room, and I'm wondering how Ivo is doing. Hopefully not bad either but who knows. Reading newspapers, watching TV, and talking with others do wonders in terms of my Croatian language. I understand almost everything from the television but when boys start talking in some kind of dialect, I am lost again. It will come for sure – *well, depending on how long I am going to stay. If 20 years, then my Croatian will be amazing.* I answer either in English or with a mix of Czech, Polish, Russian, and Croatian. Very often we are laughing about something and of course teasing each other. I'm so lucky that there are no idiots among us.

Loud bangs are coming from the room next to us. I wonder what's happening. The boys explain that it's a raid. The guards got a tip that they will find something and are now dismantling the room. One of my roommates, a drug dealer, explains that here you can trust only yourself and God. In my case, this equation is reduced to 50% as I don't believe there is a grey-haired guy in the sky who decides everything, but I keep it to myself. Many people here are devoted Christians, and I don't want to hurt anyone or get into trouble.

The TV headline news moved on from our case and is focusing on the Haag war tribunal. They just delivered a war crimes indictment of General Bobetko to the Croatian government. The media all full of the story. The boys get very angry, swear (those words I learned already) and impatiently walk around the room. As I don't have any clue, they explain that the general was in command of the Croatian army in the recent civil war; Croatians celebrate him as a hero. Everyone calms down a bit when the main TV news host explains that the government immediately rejected the charge as anti-constitutional. *In our case that probably won't happen,* I think to myself.

Split, Zatvor Bilica, Dan's cell 22nd of September 2002

Sunday. It's raining outside, a good reason to sleep the entire morning. I am so lazy that I must secretly announce another rule of my prison routine: *no fitness on Sundays!*

My mood deteriorates and all the initial excitement from writing the diary is gone. *Why? Nothing is happening!* Always the same: food, television, sleep, newspaper, food, sleep, walk, television, food, sleep… round and round. I am not sure how people manage solitary confinement; it must be one of the worst possible punishments. At least I have my mates here, all the letters that I can read over and over, and pictures of my fox. *What is she up to?* Anytime I think about her, I get very anxious that something bad will happen to her. *I must convince her to go home!*

The boys in the room start talking about why everyone is here. Vladimir was dealing cannabis and got caught. Pretty clear. Dragan was smuggling some drugs from abroad and got caught too. Nothing exciting. Both dealers talk about their past activities without emotions. Tough luck.

"What did Goran do?" I am asking. He seems a bit reserved and does not want to talk about it, but he also does not speak English, so our communication is limited.

"He killed his wife," says one of the dealers. Wow! Goran still does not say anything, just nods.

Another dealer says, "But she deserved it." Now it starts to be interesting. "She was cheating on him, he came home drunk, got in a row and he stabbed her with the kitchen knife" is the full story.

Goran seems to regret his actions but almost whispers in Croatian: "Yes, she deserved it."

"Death is a bit too much, but well, she should not cheat," concludes one of the dealers. I am not sure if I fully agree with the statement but stay quiet in order not to push any unnecessary buttons here.

What I did is clear to everyone. I am famous. It was on the front page as well as in the main TV news. The local newspaper keeps reporting on the case, but at least the story has moved away from the front pages.

"I haven't done anything, it was an accident," I explain. "No homosexuals in the boat, just a group of friends who like scuba diving and sailing. Police are trying to frame us because of the navy diver's death – that is very sad but was completely stupid, we told them they should not dive into the cave."

The boys are nodding. It's not clear what they really think but at least they don't consider me gay, with all the images of my beautiful darling next to my bed.

Split, Zatvor Bilica, Dan's cell
23rd of September 2002

Monday. A visit to the canteen is the first light moment of the day. I get ear buds, my own (plastic) cutlery, soap, Coke, and ham. This local ham is *reeeeally gooood.* Morning is spent eating and writing the journal.

After lunch, the door opens, and the guard calls my name.

"Dan, your lawyer is here."

I quickly jump out of the bed, grab my notes, the guard approves, and we walk downstairs where the meeting rooms are. I am full of expectations.

My new lawyer is here!

The lawyer shakes my hand, an older guy. He looks serious and representative. All right! No English, but it does not matter as he brought a translator: a lovely, slim woman in her fifties. She introduces herself as Jana and explains that she works as a legal translator and that Jarka stays with her, in her apartment! What a coincidence, what's the story here?

"We all met Jarka and your parents, Mr Frolec. We don't believe anything that the police came up with."

"Please call me Dan," I reply, feeling happy with how the conversation starts. *This looks really promising!*

"So, what's the situation, what's the plan?"

"Well, first of all, an extradition to the Czech Republic is out of the question – for such a crime – and it might take a lot of time to disentangle the whole case," the lawyer called Zoran explains.

"The custody in Croatia is for a maximum of six months. Within this timeframe, the state prosecutor must formally accuse you and then you wait for the court case. Alternatively, they must let you go, if there is enough evidence that you are innocent. If there is not even enough evidence to accuse you, then the judge dismisses the case."

I expected something like this, but it still feels miserable to hear it so clearly.

"Let me explain what happened on the boat." I brush off my worries and pick up my notes. *I can worry later, now it's time to focus.* "Everything is here," showing the lawyer all the arguments that we could not possibly have done such a crime. He says that he will come again this week with his assistant, and we can review everything in detail. He seems very reasonable and experienced.

"We have to leave now," Jana interrupts.

"Mrs Jana, please, convince my love to go home, I am very afraid when she is here." I probably sound very concerned.

"I will try. But tomorrow is another visit. I assume that you like her to come?"

"Of course, I am so looking forward to seeing Jarka again. Please say hi to her. I really appreciate that you take care of her, even that you host her in your house."

"No problem, she is such a sweet and intelligent lady. It's my pleasure," concludes Jana.

We shake hands and they leave, and the guard escorts me back to the room. *Finally, I've got a good lawyer. Yay!*

Evening is full of fun. Everyone buys their own *pršut*, so we are eating, laughing, talking, and farting. I have my Coke and ham and feel extraordinary. The boys keep teasing each other, for example, one of them says "intelligence coefficient" instead of "quotient", and that seems to be the joke of the month. Everyone is laughing hysterically, including the one who said it. He probably does not understand, but that's funny too! In any case, my local vocabulary is getting bigger and better.

Tonight, I realize fully for the first time that *I may stay here for quite a while. Six months as a maximum custody length! That's forever. What will happen?*

Split, Zatvor Bilica, Dan's cell
24th of September 2002

I am so tired after breakfast – from all the hard work here – that I fall asleep again. Somebody wakes me up, it's Tuesday – visits are here! I am very happy, much calmer and more balanced than the last time. *That last visit was an emotional disaster, quite untypical for me,* I am contemplating. The room with bars and the glass again. My sweetheart is coming!

We tell each other how much we love each other. That's beautiful even in such circumstances, bars and all. Then we discuss what's happening, any news, everything that should be arranged.

"I am leaving today, driving back home to Prague."

"Oh, I will miss you, but I am so happy – finally I will stop worrying about you and what can happen to you here."

"Don't worry, everything is good, people here are very helpful."

"Please don't come here again, I love you and am so happy to see you but will feel better if you are safe at home."

My plea, I feel, is useless. She seems quite determined to help me out and will come again. Well, let it be, I guess. Suddenly, the visit is ended by the guards, somewhat a wake-up call reminding me that I am on the wrong side of the bars.

"Love you."

"Love you too."

Kisses against the glass and they take me away.

Afternoon… I sleep, surprisingly, and then sweep and mop the entire room. We agreed to clean every Tuesday. It's my turn today. I normally hate these kinds of chores but here any activity is a blessing. The floor is shiny and my lower back hurts.

Lying in my bed, I contemplate the whole situation. *It's like a game! Of course, two people are dead, that's a massive tragedy but what's done is done. It seems to me that the police guys came up with a game. It's probably more interesting to accuse someone than investigate properly and discover the truth. Maybe it's a part of their job – to always suspect someone did something against the law.*

I further explore the game analogy that unfolds in my mind. *I am forced to play and can't just pass like in a poker game. Rules are not clear. There is only one option: to play. And win! Win back my freedom. After I win, I may come up with my own game. For example, suing the bloody tabloid that keeps publishing stupid, unproven stories and had revealed our full names even before any official trial started. Or… I can publish this diary, perhaps all the millions of tourists who come to Croatia every year can learn about how things really work here.*

I cut a small paper strip and write "I WILL WIN THIS GAME" and stick it inside of my cupboard with a little piece of sticky tape from the ear buds package.

How inventive one can become in jail!

My mood is very good today, unlike Vladimir's. He came back from the visit very sad and angry. I don't know what happened and he does not want to talk about it.

Evening passes slowly as I go through the arguments, evidence of our innocence that I was able to come up with. My plan of defence. Turning everything over back and forth, in order to discover anything new or any weaknesses. "*Schau unter jeden Stein*" – "look under every stone" – as one of my ex-bosses used to say. He probably did not expect that I would use his favourite saying while in custody one day. Hopefully, the lawyer will come again tomorrow, and we can discuss.

Oh, one thing, my love told me that the company chairwoman recommended that I be promoted into a much bigger job position at work.

Why? Does she consider my present experience relevant for the new job? How is this going to end up? Will they let me manage the entire Czech and Slovak company foods business from the jail? Probably not.

Split, Zatvor Bilica, Ivo's cell
25th of September 2002

Wednesday. The eleventh day of being locked up. *Feels like eternity*, Ivo thinks to himself. Days are more or less the same, the routine is quite clear now. *How is Dan doing? I am pretty calm, at least most of the time.*

Still, Ivo keeps wondering *How long are we going to be stuck here?* It looks like *Slobodna Dalmacija* daily keeps getting information straight from the police, publishing nonsense stories about homosexuals on the boat. *How come no one checks or, even worse, everyone ignores that our group is a scuba diving club on one of their regular diving trips, most of us married? My brother wrote a complaint to the Czech Ministry of Foreign Affairs, pointing out that the Croatian police investigation shows many signs of irregularities and a strange, biased approach. No reply so far...*

His thoughts are interrupted by a knock on the door and keys rattling in the lock.

"Ivo, your lawyer is here," the guard shouts.

He gathers his stuff, a couple of sheets of paper with the notes and a pen, and off they go down the corridor that he knows very well by now. Once they arrive in front of a white door leading into a special room where legal representative meetings occur, the guard lets him in, closes the door, and stays outside.

This is an uninteresting rectangular room with white walls, resembling a small classroom, with table and chairs – very different to the regular visitor's room with bars and phones. Ivo's lawyer is already here, a smart woman dressed in an elegant beige outfit, in her forties.

"Hi, Ivo, how are you doing?" the lawyer asks.

Ivo: "Not too bad, thank you. I hope you are doing well too."

"I am glad that you feel OK, given the circumstances. Listen, there are a couple of important pieces of news that I would like to share with you. I guess most of them are positive."

Wow, that sounds promising, Ivo thinks to himself, he can't wait to hear the news.

"Firstly, all your diving friends testified in front of the investigating judge and all their testimonies are aligned, none even slightly confirms the police story about motives and what happened that evening. I believe now that the police hypothesis is a fantasy and, I mean, I can't really tell with certainty, but the judge seems to be thinking the same."

Ivo interrupts her politely. "Yeah, thank you, this seems important. After all, they are all telling the truth while the police version is obviously an absurd fairy tale."

"Sure. I'll be honest with you – at the beginning I was not sure whether or not you guys are innocent. It does not happen so often that a diver gets lost in a cave, then commits suicide. However, now I am convinced that you haven't done anything and the whole incident is a tragic accident. Well, let's see what the judge's next steps are. Another piece of the puzzle that was revealed yesterday – Michael's dive computer record."

"Oh, yes, I remember the police investigators didn't want to talk about it. What does the computer show?"

"Well, it fully confirms what you and Dan kept saying. Which also means that the police theory can't be the truth. He was still alive, because the zigzag curve shows that he was looking for an exit from the cave for thirty minutes. Swimming up and down for thirty mins! Must have been an horrific experience, brr, I can't even think about it. For us though, this fact represents clear proof that you guys are innocent."

"Wow! Thank you, sounds like good news indeed! Please tell me, what is then preventing our release? Everything seems to be clear."

She continues while slightly shaking her head: "The judge still insists on waiting for the results of the DNA from the stains on the boat. The police claim that the stains are blood, it's their only remaining evidence. Contrary to what all the crew, including the captain, testified, all of them confirmed that the red stains are from a mooring rope which was used to tie in the sailboat in the Maslenica harbour."

"Hmm… well what do you recommend, anything else to be done? For how long do we have to wait?" Ivo asks rather impatiently.

"I was told that Dan's lawyer is pushing the judge to ask an official judiciary scuba diving expert to analyse the case and share his opinion. I am not sure how long this might take. For the DNA analysis, they expect the results to arrive within the next two weeks."

Ivo puts his head into his hands. "Two weeks?! Two more weeks here? What takes them so long to analyse the paint and confirm it's not blood?"

She tries to comfort him: "I am not sure, Ivo. The only option is to remain calm and patient. Our legal system is not too fast, to be honest. Many suspects wait here for months. The maximum time for custody in Croatia is six months… I hope your case will be resolved much faster but no guarantees, as you can imagine."

"Six months does not sound very promising… But on the other hand, thank you very much, all the other recent findings seems very positive. Thank you and please keep coming as much as you can – at least your visits break the monotonous routine."

She faintly smiles. She seems to like her client. "Will do. You take care of yourself, don't lose hope. I believe everything will be fine at the end."

She stands up, smiles again, shakes Ivo's hand for a little longer than is customary, and then knocks on the door. The guard waiting outside opens the door and lets her out first. She waves at Ivo, and then the guard escorts him back to the room.

What a day again! *I am thinking that the end is near but the information about the maximum custody of six months did not make me happy. But, on a positive note, my lawyer looks really beautiful… Or am I locked up for too long?*

Split, Zatvor Bilica, Dan's cell
25th of September 2002

Wednesday. Breakfast is not even finished yet and the lawyers are here. The first are the two new ones that my darling arranged. An older guy in his sixties. I learned that he is a former head of regional criminal police. He comes together with his younger assistant. I like them. The older guy is a little chubby with a balding head but has very sharp, clever eyes. His whole style with his black suit absolutely creates gravitas.

They seem quite switched on again, showing me testimonials of all my friends from the boat. Everything looks good, everything they say ties together and supports our story. *Well, the story… is the truth!* Then we go through all the arguments, all the defence points.

No blood in the boat; it was the paint from the harbour mooring.

Michael's own scuba knife, used as a weapon.

My personal dive computer showing that I was not diving and therefore could not have dropped the body into the cave. It would be very risky to dive such a dive without a computer and with an almost certainty of coming up with decompression sickness.

Lawyers claim that if there is no victim's blood on the boat or anywhere on my clothes, everything will be fine. We must wait for the results of the analysis.

How long? They don't know. It could be weeks or even months! *OMG.*

They ask me to describe all the functions and capabilities of scuba diving computers. I never realized that what seems obvious to us divers, other people have no idea about. I explain everything, like in a classroom. Both lawyers nod and the assistant takes tons of notes, saying they will have to check with the court's dive expert and explain everything to the judge.

We have spent three productive hours together; my impressions are very good. *Finally, lawyers who understand the case and are both willing and capable of learning!* They also seem to start trusting me, believing that neither Ivo nor myself have done anything like what the police are suggesting. All good.

A couple of minutes after their departure, another lawyer is here: the one that was arranged by the consul, who did not understand anything. He is trying hard to keep the case, understanding that I engaged other lawyers. Well, let's give him a chance too. Anyway, the Czech government seems to be paying for his services, at least so far. Unlike the new lawyer, he speaks English very well, therefore our conversation is easier. He has more information about the entire process and all the procedures that the investigation involves. We speak for an hour, but the key conclusion is the same: if there is no blood, there is no case. From his experience, such analysis can take four to five months.

WTF! I could be stuck here for another five months?! Hard to believe.

I decide to keep him too. More lawyers, more chances of figuring out something. The main topic will be trying to find out if there is any chance of speeding up the slow process of evidence analysis and the overall bureaucratic decision-making apparatus. Let's see. What can be done will be done and rest is in the stars.

My mood is super upbeat after the lawyer meetings. Partly because there is a light at the end of the tunnel (except for five months…), partly because any distraction from the routine jail life is more than welcome.

My afternoon consists of analysing all the defence arguments again, searching for any hole, any cracks as well as writing down a kind of scuba computer guide for beginners. Any meaningful activity here is great, keeps your mind busy. Otherwise, what's left? Looking at the ceiling or watching the TV. Neither of these activities are my favourite, to be honest.

I must come up with another activity to keep my mind occupied! Maybe better learning English? Or Croatian? Well, that somehow happens anyway.

Evening arrives, and I start writing the diary. All of sudden, loud sounds of a brawl come from the neighbouring cell. Then banging, sounds of boots stomping in the corridor. We all try to listen to everything as much as we can. What an excitement! Most likely a brawl between two roommates. We hear from the corridor that the guards are asking others what happened. No one knows.

"I don't know."

"I was doing my crossword."

"I was watching TV."

"We don't know, we haven't seen anything."

One of the jail rules kicks in. No one will say anything that could affect other roommates. The guards will have to sort it out. My friends say that won't be a problem – both prisoners are going into solitary confinement.

There is plenty of time to think about what happened. Apparently one of your hands is tied to a wooden plank-bed. That piece of wood is the only thing in the room. *Even though I usually enjoy, even search for, new experiences – I hope that this one will be avoided.*

Split, Zatvor Bilica, Dan's cell
26th of September 2002

Rainy day. Awesome! It means we all sleep through the entire day. The only two earth-shattering events of today are a visit from the jail director and a walk to the canteen. I buy some postcards of Split town. My roommates are laughing, saying that I am a tourist here. That's technically correct! I will write to the friends and family, something like, *Greetings from holidays in Croatia, it's beautiful and sunny here.* Hopefully my parents will get the joke…

The war-crime process with Milosevic starts in Hague today, transmitted live by the Croatian television channel. Milosevic was a president of former Yugoslavia and later Serbia, one of the key people who started the wars against Bosnia and Croatia. The boys are listening to his opening speech and shaking their heads in disbelief. I don't know much about their past, still-quite-recent wars, but on a positive note it seems that my Croatian is getting significantly better as I understand most of what's being said.

Split Harbour, on board of *Domani*
26th of September 2002

The mood on board the sailboat is ecstatic! The boys are going home! Yesterday, the police brought their passports, and they were told that they can go back to Czech Republic.

Even though everyone is concerned about their two friends in the jail and still very sad about the death of their scuba friend, obviously those feelings are now overridden by the happiness that the waiting is finally over.

Pike stays in Croatia; he has another group arriving next week. Let's see if they come. Everyone back home of course knows the story from the main TV news.

They say farewell and agree to meet soon back in Prague, in one of the usual pubs to honour his deceased friend with a couple of drinks. The car door closes and off they go.

The captain slowly unties the boat and leaves the coast guard mooring behind. He can't stand to stay here a single minute longer. Anywhere around the beautiful Croatian coast will be much better.

Sails up, again.

Split, Zatvor Bilica, Dan's cell
27th of September 2002

Today should be without any major events, therefore I am ordering myself rest and relaxation. I will sleep as much as possible, to catch up after last night in front of the telly, watching the Hague tribunal. As soon as breakfast is gobbled up, I fall asleep. Someone wakes me up right away.

What? I am little disoriented.

"Your lawyer is here," says the guard standing at the door. All right. I climb down the bunk and get ready. Hopefully there is no bad news!

"Welcome, Dan, how are you doing? All good in jail? Must be hard but you look well rested and somehow happy."

"Yeah, I am getting used to it," I reply with a grin. I'm not sure what my body language communicates, but I feel quite good. "Hopefully, I won't be needing to get used to the prison cell for much longer. What do you think?"

"Our case has developed in a rather positive direction, Dan. They found lots of nitrogen in Michael's blood. Obviously, you know what it means but our dive expert had to explain it to the judge." The lawyer smiles a bit, he must be accustomed to talking about stuff like this without any emotions. Then, he continues. "Michael must have been underwater in rather significant depth for a long time leading up to his death. The results are still unofficial but for sure lean the case on a suicide."

Now, I can't suppress lighting up too. "Sure. That's what we all kept telling the police over and over. They simply did not want to listen."

Zoran nods. "Yes, but we know their objective was always to accuse you. They selected evidence that was suitable to their story and overlooked anything against it. Quite unprofessional, I must say."

"Hmm, well, that's clear now but I guess it's getting clearer and clearer every day that we are innocent. What do you think?" My voice probably shows a combination of hope, impatience, and fear, all at the same time.

"Listen, I don't want to give you false hopes. Judicial machine works somewhat slowly here. If all goes well, you will be released as soon as negative analysis of that paint, which police claims to be blood, comes in."

I feel excited but try to manage my feelings.

What if it really takes five months? I have been here for almost two weeks today and it already feels like an eternity...

We shake hands and bid farewell; my mood is great anyway. Everything has started to fall into place.

The rest of the day is really R & R. I sleep, and have fish for lunch. Did I say how surprised I was about the food quality and taste here? Then showers. I put on fresh clothes and the whole world feels somewhat brighter.

After dinner we talk about Croatian politics and the war. For us in the Czech Republic, war is so difficult to imagine, but for Croatians it is very vivid still. The Croatian war of independence occurred between 1991 and 1995, just a couple of years ago! I understand what they talk about but can't fully comprehend as I have never in my life experienced anything like that. One of the mates was in the battle as a member of the Croatian army. He speaks about walking in the villages not being sure from where the bullet will come. This is nuts! My whole situation somewhat pales if one imagines what people went through here.

One of the guards brings me a letter. Yay! From my love! It took the letter eight days to arrive, hence everything is probably history by now. My darling writes from Prague, saying that she's trying to move the case to the Czech Republic. I now feel that it might make sense to finish everything here. Let's see.

Split, Zatvor Bilica, Dan's cell
28th of September 2002

Weekend. Usually, the worst days here. Nothing happens! Time really slows down and runs like an old turtle. We sleep most of the day. In the afternoon, my mind starts playing tricks with me and tries to pull me down.

What if I will be stuck here for several months? What if my darling leaves me? What if...? Stupid.

I try to concentrate, breathe to stop such negative thoughts but today it's not working out very well.

Sounds of the football game are coming from outside, from the jail courtyard. It reminds me that I should write a note to the floor commander – to give me back the laces. A pair of sneakers was sent to me by my parents, but the guards took out the laces. I can walk but no running, hence no football.

The only thing besides my negative thoughts which really starts bothering me is smoking. Two of the guys in the room smoke and everything flies up towards the ceiling where my bed is. Nothing to be done, I simply must get used to it. Or start smoking?

All right, let's stop stupid thoughts and really look inside and summarize how I feel after two weeks in the jail:

1. I don't miss work.

2. I don't miss alcohol, perhaps except for a bit of red wine.

3. I exercise and breathe every day, it feels great.

4. I don't have enough aerobic activity: running or swimming.

5. I feel very well rested.

6. I never feel that slight unidentifiable pressure inside my head that I sometimes feel at work. Probably from the laptop and mobile phone screens.

7. I miss my parents and mainly my darling!

8. I like comfort and luxury but can be very happy without them. Or I can create luxury from small things, like Coke, vitamins, or one Tic Tac bonbon per day.

9. I can eat anything; it does not matter.

10. One must do something or will go nuts. Maybe meditation can help?

11. Axel Munthe: "Animals are more important than people" (I always thought so too).

12. What matters: love, travel, experiencing novelty and inspiration. It's even better with someone you either love or enjoy being with, to share the experience.

Split, Zatvor Bilica, Dan's cell
29th of September 2002

In the morning, someone comes and pours disinfectant into our toilet. It smells so bad. Vladimir, the drug dealer who was in the war, doesn't like it and sprays water everywhere without asking anyone. Dragan, the other drug dealer, wants the disinfectant to keep working and challenges Vladimir. Words fly around, our first major conflict! So far so good, the boys calm down. The whole toilet corner is full of water. When anyone goes there they bring water all around the room and make a mess.

I feel that I should not pay attention to silly issues, but it feels like Vladimir might create trouble. He doesn't talk to me much and starts to attack the other inmates in our room.

During the walk outside, Dragan looks around. He sees that Vladimir sits in a distance on the other side of the courtyard. He walks slowly, sits next to me on a concrete ledge, and starts whispering in his broken English.

"Did you notice Vladimir's reaction to the toilet issue? He is mad!"

"Yeah, I did, thought it best not to get involved. What are you thinking?"

"He is crazy, I know that he killed several people during the war and I feel that his brain is a bit of mess," continues Dragan while looking around to check Vlad is not anywhere close by.

Dragan is the only really sane and intelligent person in our room; hence, I feel it's good to make a little alliance here. "Hmm, difficult. I see your point, hundred percent. But what should we do? I mean, we are stuck with him."

"I heard that he gossips about us with some of the lads from the other rooms. Indeed, better if you don't get involved as you are a foreigner and Vladimir is unpredictable." Dragan scratches his ear while thinking. "Let me try to handle him in case of any issues in future. But, of course, if there is a fight – we have to stick with each other and have a good, consistent story for the guards."

I give a subtle nod. "Yes, done deal. Thanks for bringing it up, Dragan."

"Time is up, line up and back to the rooms!" shouts the guard, and our discussion is over.

The water in the cell has evaporated, the room looks tidy, everyone pretends like nothing happened. Good.

The television shows a nature documentary, and there is one of my favourite animals – a dugong! Any moment for mood improvement must be harvested fully.

Split, Zatvor Bilica, Dan's cell
30th of September 2002

I did not know anything this morning, but today, Monday, is going to be full of exciting events. Canteen, walk, showers, maybe even a lawyer's visit. *And right, he is here!* I am curious which one of my legal team…

Guards take me down; they are very relaxed today – I can take all my notes with me. In the room is my preferred lawyer, ex-criminal police guy, together with the translator. I feel very happy. Let's see what comes up. They say that I could be out in ten days! *Wow.* I don't believe it. This is just to manage my expectations, but it's good news anyway.

Lunch is not amazing: some kind of intestines; my food goes to the boys. I buy some mini croissants filled with wine cream in the canteen instead. What a day!

After the walk, guards bring me books from my darling. FINALLY! Books are here! It took some time. The judge probably had to read them all to find out if there is anything strange. Like how to cut the bars or something.

Little Prince by Saint-Exupéry, one of our lovebirds' favourite books, goes under the pillow. How romantic. *The Tibetan Book of the Dead*, oh my god, really? The next one: the trilogy *The Lord of the Rings*, I love it. I'm starting to read the Tibetan one, right after the prologue

– the guards are here again, interrupting my encounter with death. Showers. There is always something today, such a busy day compared to the boring weekend.

After showers, the collection of dirty laundry. A very sophisticated method. Everyone puts their laundry into a plastic bag with a little paper stripe with their name and a list of items. Guards call us one by one to the corridor to check the bag and take it over.

Another event! It never ends today. Doctor's visit. He comes and brings medication to those who have prescriptions. Two of the boys from our room take anti-depressants. One must put the pill inside of his mouth and swallow in front of the doc and the guard. Today there is an innovation – the physician crushes the tablet so it cannot be hidden under the tongue and later sold to other people. Anti-depressants have a huge value here. Very clever. The boys are seriously angry; nobody likes the pills. I am laughing, no meds for me, thank you. *Not yet?*

Split, Zatvor Bilica, Dan's cell
1st of October 2002

They still don't want to give my sneaker laces back to me. What a shame! No running during the regular walks, at least not yet.

But inventive geniality in the jail has no limits. One of my mates cuts off the handles from a plastic bag and we use them as laces. Done! The walk is at 8am today (disaster to wake up so early), but I could try my new 'laces'. Running around the small square courtyard surrounded by walls on each side feels a little stupid; nevertheless, it works! It's quite cold today, hard to guess, maybe 10°C, but the pleasure of running is immense.

I was told that my parents will come today for a visit. Let's see. In the prison, one never knows what comes up even though paradoxically life is quite routine.

A guard opens the door. "Dan has a visit," he says, and I can't wait to see if my folks really made it all the way to Croatia.

They are here! Guards allowed both my dad and mum to join, which is quite unusual – normally, it's only one person per visit, but perhaps they realized that they live far away, and my behaviour is good so far.

Happiness generated by seeing my loved ones is incredible. I almost feel serotonin being injected by my brain into the body. I also feel quite relaxed, which probably makes them chilled too even though they obviously seem a bit nervous; bars and guards and other prisoners, nothing they have ever experienced, I guess. We virtually hug each other and start talking.

"We love you so much, Daniku." My dad addresses me with a name which they used when I was a little child. It feels beautiful.

Mum, who is quite matter-of-fact, continues: "Many people are working day and night on resolving this crazy situation. Everyone back in Czech supports you and Ivo."

"That's so nice to hear. I hear that the biggest TV channel, Nova, apparently sent investigative journalists to Croatia to find out what the case is about. Is it the truth, did they really send a team?"

Dad jumps in: "Yes, correct, they spoke to us. You are already famous, now we might be too." He cracks a joke, and I am so happy to see that they are not worried. Or at least not desperate.

We talk some more, but 15 minutes just fly by. How short it feels when you see your loved ones while behind bars!

"We love you, keep strong," my dad says. That's when emotions overcome me and I can't say much, all our eyes are wet, and the visit is over.

Eighteen days in jail today. What a mess anyway.

Trust is important now, I keep telling myself, *trust that everything will work out just fine and this whole thing will soon become an incredible experience.* Sometimes I manage to convince myself, other times doubts cloud my mind. *What if the Croatians really manage to sentence us? What if they can manipulate the indisputable evidence that none of us could have killed Michael? Who knows?*

Another interesting consequence of this seemingly positive case developments is… that I don't have enough topics to keep my brain occupied. Up until recently, I was busy (as much as one can be in the jail) with sorting out all the facts, turning them around, identifying different alternative approaches to defence, thinking about 'the enemy in the wargame' – criminal police – and what kind of nonsense they may be able to come up with and any possible arguments against it. *Of course, I know that Michael committed suicide after running out of air in the depth of the cave. I know the truth! But, will it really come out?*

Fewer things to think about mean that I will have to come up with something else because boredom slowly starts to set in. Yes, I've got the books, that's amazing as I always loved reading. *What else? Let's try to come up with some kind of meditation. I have never really done anything like that but why not start?* Many people claim that meditation brings a lot of benefits. *But how to go about it? I have no idea but let's try.*

I slowly breathe in and imagine collecting energy from the entire universe, channelling it through an imaginary funnel into my nostrils. As the air filled with that space, energy enters my body, it changes into a stream of small bubbles, and I direct those bubbles into different parts of my body one by one. First the right side: feet, calf, thigh, swap to left feet, calf, thigh, move to pelvis, belly, spine, all the muscles around the spine, chest, heart, lungs, left arm, right arm, finish with the skull and its contents. Each body part, one slow inhale and slow exhale. I imagine that the stream of the bubbles is entering each part and regenerating all the cells on inhale. Then, collecting any trash, any particles, anything that should be removed and carrying those into my lungs and out on exhale.

Honestly, I am not sure it's working but for sure it kills time! Who knows, perhaps this NEW SPACE MEDITATION will make me famous one day…

The interpersonal situation in our cell is developing in an interesting direction. The guy who started to bother me somehow calmed down, so I decided to ignore his occasional provocations and share with him everything as if nothing had happened. I am not sure why he changed his behaviour towards me but at least he behaves normally except teasing one of the other guys from time to time.

Another exciting moment today! A full search of the neighbouring room. They probably look for drugs. We obviously hear everything, all the noises, banging of batons, shouting. My mates explain that such a search entails throwing everything out of the cell by the prisoners and then guards will thoroughly inspect every square inch of the room. I feel that one day it will happen to our room too. Regular control of my small cupboard became a routine for me – to check that nothing 'strange', no pills, materialized inside, out of thin air.

Split, Zatvor Bilica, Ivo's cell
1st of October 2002

Start of the new month. *What will October bring?* Ivo is lying on his bunk, reading the *Slobodna Dalmacija* newspaper. At least they stopped writing about the case on the front page – it was unbearable to read all the police fantasies every day. Obviously, all the guys in the room read it too, nothing pleasant.

Ivo is thinking to himself:

Seventeen days behind the bars... Who would have thought it will happen to me? Definitely not myself. Now the reality is here and it's somewhat strange how well I seem to cope.

Ivo's daily routine: reading newspapers, watching TV, learning Croatian, regular food – quite good, he thinks – walk outside, showers, canteen, meeting with lawyers, various discussions with roommates. *It's bearable so far.* Obviously, that's because he trusts that the truth will be revealed, and they will let Dan and him go.

How is Dan doing? Ivo's lawyer said Dan is all right, and he changed his lawyer. Apparently the new one is much better, more experienced. Hopefully they can together manage to convince the judge about the truth.

Hard to imagine... what if they manage to frame us and throw us into a real prison? Maximum sentence for murder in Croatia is 40 years. Let's say I 'get away' with 20. Twenty years of life taken away from me for a crime that I haven't committed. Indeed, hard to imagine. Better not think too much. Still… there are many people in this world who are unjustly imprisoned. Now I know how they might feel. Awful.

All this chatter in my mind is not helping. Let's focus on something more useful and memorize the Croatian words from our room discussion yesterday…

Split, Zatvor Bilica, Dan's cell
2nd of October 2002

Wake up, brush teeth, breakfast, showers, walk, work out, bed, reading, nap, lunch, reading, nap, stretching, basketball match on TV, *I still wonder how come there is a telly in the jail?* … dinner, diary writing, evening news, my meditation and breathing exercises, reading, more telly, lights out. A full day of events…

Still one thing stands out – Croatian TV shows *The Simpsons* in the evening. We are laughing so hard that my whole belly and diaphragm hurt. We are also banging our metal cups on the table. Lots of fun.

Split, Zatvor Bilica, Dan's cell
3rd of October 2002

The jail starts to annoy me. Luckily, I began reading a new book. Unfortunately, I read so fast that I finish it in one day.

Lawyers were here too, all good news, but we must be patient.

Bloody hell, I have already been patient for 20 days here!

We have to wait.

I don't want to wait! I want to go home!

They say a couple more days. Well, let's see.

The whole situation can develop in various directions. I trust that we will get out, regain our freedom, but I am resisting to believe in 'a couple more days' so as not to go nuts if it does not happen.

What keeps my love busy? And what about my parents? It must be so hard for them – knowing that I am stuck here and not able to help in any meaningful way. My friends? It's evening both here and back home. Everyone is probably watching TV at home. Same here, with one subtle difference – I am watching TV in jail.

An interesting thought crosses my mind: *How many people are now unjustly imprisoned around the world, sitting in jail for a crime that they haven't committed?*

In the morning, Dragan asked the guards for his old shoelaces that are stored somewhere in the building.

We did not understand why but he got them with the evening guard visit.

"What are they for, Dragan?" asks Goran. "Will you follow Dan's example and start running?"

"Don't be silly. No one else would be so stupid to run around the courtyard. Except for our Dan here." He turns towards me with a smile and gives me the laces. "They are for you, so that you can run even faster."

The boys start laughing. Me too. I am really touched though, and did not expect such a selfless act of generosity.

"Thanks a lot, Dragan, I am so happy! Let me put them in."

Taking out the previous solution, plastic bag handles, takes some effort, but soon my sneakers look like they got new life.

"Fantastic, thanks again. What are the guards going to say at the walk when they notice?" I am not sure about such things.

"They will never notice," Vladimir says. "They don't really pay attention, unless someone starts a fight."

The night falls slowly. The Mediterranean air is still pleasantly warm. I feel very happy with my new shoelaces and even more so that our room seems to have reached a state of harmony and mutual respect. Much better than fighting.

Split, Zatvor Bilica, Dan's cell
4th of October 2002

My dad's name day is today. One of the boys in our room has the same name, so I give him chocolate that I bought in the canteen a couple of days ago. He is very happy, sharing with everybody, probably did not expect anything. I am happy too. Such a small gesture of kindness makes the day for everyone here.

Afternoon. Another visit, this time the pretty consul Vera. All good apparently, everyone is doing whatever possible to help us out. Nothing new but any visit breaks the routine and brings more fun than being stuck in the cell.

During the hour and a half outside, I walk for an hour and run for 30 minutes. It feels so good! All the other prisoners are having fun and teasing me, but I don't care. The laces remain unnoticed.

Split, Zatvor Bilica, Dan's cell
5th of October 2002

My dad's birthday. I forgot to wish him well.

But how to do it? How to wish someone a happy birthday, or anything else really, if you are in jail. Assuming of course, that the other person is not in the same jail, in the same room with you. Even if my dad was here too, there is no way to contact other mates. Well, he will have to survive without my wishes.

I am guessing that the most precious present would be my freedom, but we will have to wait for that.

Split, Zatvor Bilica, Dan's cell
6th of October 2002

My darling visited today! She looked a bit sad though. *I want to go home! I want to be with her! The thought of her being worried about me is horrible. Bloody police bastards! Why me?* Obviously, my day is not great today, my mood is somewhat dark. Peculiar.

What did I do in my previous life that I deserve this kind of shit?

Some people say that everything you do will return to you. Good and bad. *Did I do anything bad?* I'm not sure but it would be interesting if such a concept really works and it's not just some kind of religious blabbering to keep the faithful in check.

To add to my built-up frustration, the smoking of one of the boys is really getting on my nerves. Even my lungs are in pain from time to time, but it must be psychological. I don't believe that passive smoking can have such a physical effect. *What to do? Probably nothing, just work with my mind to get rid of the feeling of frustration. Convincing him to stop? Well, that's like wishing to become a fly and fly away through the window bars.*

I notice that every negative thought impacts my overall wellbeing, my mental state.

I must learn to control my mind and thoughts!

One positive item on the list today: I wrote a speech to present to the media after they release us from here. *Should I laugh at myself? What if everyone outside has already forgotten? Or, what if we are never going to get out?*

Split, Zatvor Bilica, Dan's cell
7th of October 2002

Terrible day! Lots of work. Wake-up call, breakfast, lawyer #1, shop visit, lunch, lawyer #2, fresh-air walk, TV watching, showers, dirty laundry preparation, dinner, dirty laundry handover to the guards, change of bedsheets. We are so exhausted! *How can all these people outside manage their daily lives with 1,000 times more stuff happening?*

Meeting with the lawyers went reasonably well. I only really care about what Mr Zoran says; he seems really switched on. No wonder, for a former criminal police chief.

"We don't have much news today, Dan," he starts the conversation after we shake hands. His beautiful young assistant just smiles and shakes my hand too. It's nice to feel a woman's touch, to be honest.

"Everyone keeps waiting for the sample analysis from the investigation centre in the capital. The judge won't decide anything until he is sure that there is nothing suspicious."

"Sure, I get it," I interrupt rather impatiently, "but for how long do we still have to wait? Is there any way to speed it up?"

The lawyer shakes his head. "I have to disappoint you here, I am afraid. The investigators take their time, there is nothing we can do here."

"All right, I get it. I must be patient. However, it's not so easy – as you can imagine. Also," I switch topic, "I am seriously concerned that something happens to my girlfriend here. What do you think? She doesn't want to listen to me and keeps staying in Croatia."

"Don't worry, Dan, she is safe. Our country can be a little bit crazy, people too emotional and so on, but no one will do anything to her, trust me." He seems really convinced, and the assistant nods too.

"All right then, it is what it is. Thanks a lot for coming to see me. Do we have anything else to discuss, please?"

"In my view, the forensic results will arrive by the end of this week and then everything will be sorted out," Zoran finishes. We shake hands again – with the assistant too of course – and I call the guard to escort me back to the room. *The guard likes her too but can't shake her hand, tough luck,* I think to myself but obviously say nothing.

I was going to order a pair of nail clippers from the shop but *what if they let me go before the order comes in? Well, let's not jinx the whole thing. I am ordering.*

My mood is much better today. It must be the thought of *everything will be sorted out by the weekend.* I even caught myself feeling that I am in some kind of kids' summer camp. There are rules which must be followed (more or less), daily routine, regular meals, repetitive activities… I really liked summer camps when I was a kid.

One thing is missing though – girls!

One of the guards knocks on the door and gives me back my shoelaces and the leather belt. *What's happening? Either I behaved well, and they trust me now, or they want me to hang myself…*

Split, Zatvor Bilica, Dan's cell
8th of October 2002

Today is the visit day, my fox will come! The commander has authorized an extended visit, so we've got 30 minutes. With the unbreakable glass between, of course. Finally, we have more time to talk! Not only about the necessary arrangement and legal strategies but also about how we miss each other, how we love each other, how Oskar (her cat at home, which now feels like *ours*) is doing and so on. I am very happy and sad at the same time. Happy to talk but sad because it makes me feel even more intensely how much I want to get out of here. Hug, kiss my darling. And more.

'Miss Stubborn' obviously came up with a different plan than to go back to Prague.

"While I am wasting my time with you here," she says with a smile and a wink, "perhaps I can do something fun too."

"All right, what is it? I want to do something fun too…"

"The captain has a week free before another group comes over from Czech, so he invited me to sail around the Dalmatian coast for a couple of days. I think I will take him up on the offer even though water is not my element as you know."

"Wow, that's sounds fantastic. Shall I be jealous?" I react with a smile. She knows that I don't mean it seriously. Pike is a good friend, and she deserves a bit of a holiday after all the stuff happening around me.

"Don't be silly, darling. I love you, otherwise I would not be here in the first place." She shakes her head which results in her lovely brown hair flying around before settling back on her shoulders. So beautiful!

"I know, I know. I love you too. Enjoy the sailing and see you next week then." I pretend to be sad, but I am so happy for her, and happy that I can have such a beautiful and smart human being close to me.

Later, back in the room, I lie on my bunk and contemplate the future. *Are we going to stay together? Is this relationship really what it seems to be, i.e. a love to last a lifetime? How are we going to settle back into a 'normal life' after all this?*

My thoughts are interrupted by another, this time unusual piece of prison routine. A visit from the prison commander! He seems to be a nice guy, asks us how we are doing, praising us for our tidy cell. Pity he did not bring some diplomas; I would hang mine above my bed. One of the boys shows him a flattened earwig claiming that he got bitten on his genitals last night. This, in my view a *rather unbelievable story*, should be supporting our plea for a pest control action. The commander does not show any signs of distrust and promises to organize something. I hope that we will survive such an event.

The Lord of the Rings volume three is finished and thus I have nothing to read. *What's left to amuse myself? TV and this damned diary.* It's quite useful. I just managed to kill two mosquitos with it that were happily sitting on the ceiling and waiting for lights out to suck my blood.

Split, Zatvor Bilica, Dan's cell
9th of October 2002

When I start writing about today's event, I realize something extraordinary.

Physically, I haven't felt so well for ages! I am well rested, with a great amount of good sleep. I am happy with every, or at least most mornings, fresh-air walk where I always manage to run around the courtyard. I exercise daily in the room, I breathe well, eat reasonably tasting food regularly. I have almost no stress, at least not that persistent time-constrain stress of managing everything life and work bring. Of course, I miss my family and my love. Honestly, I miss sex too, but it can be managed. Oh, and no alcohol! This must be the key reason for all these clear, bright mornings. One more thing! No electronics, no screens! My mind is very often peaceful here.

There is a faint feeling that this prison experience might have a profound influence on my future life. On what's important (and what isn't). How I spend my time. Chasing stupid things that clearly one does not need to be happy. Stressing out at work.

At the moment, I don't have any clear idea what to do differently, but I feel that something will for sure happen.

What is truly important in life? Success at work? Money? Power to influence stuff? Reading bloody emails for two hours every day? Social mixers that I don't want to attend? Dinners in expensive restaurants? Developing and launching a new product? Regular doses of stress?

Or time with the people I love? Peace of mind? Physical and mental health and wellbeing? Meet new, interesting people? Sit by the sea and just listen to the sound of the waves?

Written so clearly next to each other, it's super obvious what's better, isn't it?

Hopefully, I will remember this day and thoughts while sitting behind my desk in my beautiful modern office, staring at the screen with my eyes, back, and wrists hurting.

Tonight, we started a cell conversation about the birth of the universe and the start of life on Earth. Given my Croatian proficiency, or lack of it, the value of our scientific-theological discussion is rather questionable.

Vladimir, our war hero, was reading something in the newspaper which made him start the debate: "Folks, I hope it's clear to everyone that our universe and everything in it was created by almighty God. Do you agree, what do you think?"

Dragan rolls his eyes in disbelief. "How on earth can you think anything like that. There is a ton of evidence that the universe started with the Big Bang. All the galaxies moving away from each other. Neutrinos which are hard to observe but originated in that event. Tons of evidence."

"But," jumps in Goran, "I believe in God. Do you think that God does not exist?"

I feel that this might be a dangerous direction so for now decide to stay quiet.

"No, no, that's not what I said." Dragan waves his hand in the air like he wants the idea to go away. "God might or might not exist, that's a different question. What I say is that we can believe in God but that does not mean he created the universe."

"So, what about us and all the animals and plants?" counters Vlad. "Do you think they just appeared out of nowhere?"

Now I can't resist. "Have you read the Darwin theory of evolution? In my mind there is little doubt that life's origin has been a coincidence of suitable conditions on this planet and then evolution took care of the rest. Just look at all the excavations, different species on remote islands, evolution of humans from apes to Neanderthals to Homo sapiens."

Dragan keeps nodding while I express my view. He and I clearly have similar ideas on the topic.

"You too don't believe in God, Dan?" asks Goran, turning to myself, in no way aggressive but clearly interested in a view that might be so different from his own.

"Let me explain. I don't believe there is a guy in Heaven with a long white beard, who controls everything and decides about faith of all of us. If he, or she, is so powerful, it would be too boring to be busy with our meaningless little lives." I try to tread carefully, while still speaking my mind. "I feel that there is some unexplainable energy, something that connects our universe, you can call it consciousness if you like. But the guy with white beard? No."

"Hmm… what about Heaven and Hell and so on, do you guys feel there is something like that?" asks Goran. Vladimir seems to be immersed in his thoughts. Perhaps he did not expect such conversation.

"In my view, this is a church fairy tale to keep people in line and obeying the authorities," says Dragan. "If you are good, you will go to Heaven. If you are bad, you will go to Hell. What does it mean, 'be good'? Obey what the priest or your lord tells you? Give them your wife? Work hard on their fields? Bollocks. Just a tool to manage common people." He seems rather passionate about the subject.

Goran puts his head into his hands and there is a moment of silence. Vlad says nothing. He clearly disagrees but does not have more good arguments to support his view. Finally, Goran looks up and to my big surprise says, "Thank you, guys. This Hell–Heaven thing never made sense to me and now I feel rather at peace. It looks like I can believe in God and at the same time don't trust all the nonsense which we keep hearing from the Catholic priests."

"Fair enough, Goran. I am happy that you are happy." I feel that moving away from an argument into some kind of balanced compromise is the right thing to do here. "Indeed, not an easy topic to talk about. Moreover, who knows what the truth really is, to be honest."

Our debate reaches a stage of discussing a possibility of multiple, multi-dimensional parallel universes including God. This option somehow exceeds both our theoretical knowledge as well as my local vocabulary though.

I decide to move my attention to more productive activities and after watching *The Simpsons* start reading the third book of *The Lord of the Rings* again. Saruman was just kicked out by the elf army. He is not happy.

Finishing the day with my *space meditation* has become regular practice now. I am so grateful that something simple like that came my way. This will be probably one of the lifetime learnings from here.

Split, Zatvor Bilica, Dan's cell
10th of October 2002

The only bright moment of today is drawing our cell scheme. Very good work. (Feel free to have a look at page no. 164.)

For the rest of the day, I can't stop thinking about my darling and worrying. *She is on the sailing boat, weather sucks with strong wind and rain, big waves out there for sure! She can't swim... What a mess. 'Sranje' they say here. Possibly at the sea, who knows, but in my mind too.*

I must find a better way to manage my thoughts.

What comes to mind is how I sorted myself out when my former girlfriend that I had met in Moscow gave me the boot. I was 19. She was absolutely gorgeous, and we were together, loving each other for more than a year. Then, back in Prague, she told me that she met another guy. I was very sad on the way back home after that terrible conversation, crying while sitting in the tube train. Hearing one of the stations in the Prague city centre, I realized that I was very close to my favourite bar, Arcadia if I recall well. I got out at the last moment before the train doors slammed shut, went upstairs into the bar, ordered a double Johnny Walker Black Label on the rocks, and contemplated life. What a big deal?! There are so many other girls. Let's not be sad, let's celebrate my freedom! That moment will remain with me forever, as one of the great memories. How to twist a seemingly bad situation into a celebration just using my mind (and whisky).

Remember this story, Dan, and stop worrying! Everything is and will be all right.

Split, Zatvor Bilica, Dan's cell
11th of October 2002

Tomorrow at 5pm will elapse the duration of my custody as decided by the judge. If we don't receive another decision about its prolongation – *I go home!* Both lawyers were here, and both say that the custody will be extended. Let's see.

I hope that the Croatian administrative machine is not perfect, and they forget to prolong it. That would be awesome. Call the guards at 17:05 tomorrow and tell them to prepare all my stuff because I am leaving.

The day flows as normal; I am used to the jail rhythm by now. The difference is that every noise of a key turning in the door lock makes me jump today.

It's 9pm and still nothing. One of the boys is in the same situation. We are already planning a joint trip to the Split streets.

Oh shit!

At 21:30, the guard opens the door and calls me out, into the corridor. The boys are laughing.

Obviously, I get the custody extension paper. Another month. I return inside, and the door closes behind me. My friend claps his hands. Nothing for him? Another key rattle, and he goes out. "There is mail for you," says the guard and we laugh again. The guard too. So, no Split nightlife. At least not tomorrow.

Split, Zatvor Bilica, Dan's cell
12th of October 2002

While describing a list of prison advantages, I mentioned the TV. What remains to be revealed is so-called Channel 8.

This is a jail video channel!

We can watch several standard TV Croatia channels or this Channel 8. Every day, at 3pm and 8pm, they play different movies, probably from VHS (google it if you don't know what it means). The movies are often very interesting and valuable, often in the original English with local subtitles. For example, last week we had a movie full of blood about crossbreeding humans with sharks. The story does not deserve further elaboration, unfortunately.

But today is a movie festival! Croatian TV shows one of the Indiana Jones today, followed by *Starship Troopers*. Enough writing, let's get to watching!

Split, Zatvor Bilica, Dan's cell
13th of October 2002

Today marks one month in jail. There is a mass today, let me join the boys. *No, I haven't become a religious fanatic here. However, I am very curious.* There is a mass once a fortnight, somewhere inside the prison building. Let's go.

The chapel is right next to the shop, the same door type as all the cells. The whole ceremony is in Croatian, but I understand almost everything. One month here clearly worked, at least to learn the language. My focus switches from the priest monologue to my thoughts about God.

If he exists – which I doubt but do not fully dismiss – is he aware about my profound disrespect for the church, the institution that 'represents' him here? If yes, he so far has decided not to inform me.

As I sit in the first row, the priest comes closer to us and shakes my hand, wishing me peace. I wear long pants and normal shoes after a long time. For some reason I feel like a normal human, instead of a prisoner. Nice. I am happy that I joined. As a reward, I continue my day by sleeping until lunch.

The TV news report about terrorist attacks in Bali, one of the tropical paradise islands. *One to visit in future,* I reckon.

It seems to me that the world is increasingly being divided into 'Islamist' and 'non-Islamist'. One of the key questions of the future and prosperity of human civilization might therefore be how to identify good Muslims and let them be, and how to find the bad guys and eliminate them. Perspective failure of this concept will eventually lead into a complete isolation of Muslim countries, including Muslim minorities in the rest of the world. The only solution must be that 'good' Muslims will wake up and eliminate the terrorists themselves. Well, let's see.

I want to visit Indonesia next year! Perhaps this dilemma will be addressed by a continuing holiday in Croatian jail?

Good night.

Split, Zatvor Bilica, Dan's cell
14th of October 2002

Today's events are being recorded with a one-day delay. Nothing extraordinary happened anyway, perhaps except for an incident at the fresh-air walk.

One of the mates kept provoking me, calling me gay, trying to catch my hand and touch me. He is probably gay himself and can't really show it, here in the homophobic Croatian society. I did not let him do anything, but at the same time did not create a big drama. I just shoved him a bit and that was enough. One never knows, he always seems to be talking to the guards, and I am the foreigner here.

Better keep my head down, under the radar screens.

In any case, I feel somewhat angry and uncertain too – *what do I do if he repeats this behaviour again? I will probably hit him in the jaw or call guards for help. Hitting him is dangerous; what if other mates support him? Calling guards is cowardly, which could create a wrong image here. Let's see. I will probably hit him hard. The only thing I want are no issues and to go home.*

No news from lawyers today. When???

Split, Zatvor Bilica, Dan's cell
15th of October 2002

Tuesday, visit day!

My fox will come if she obviously hasn't drowned in the sea. I asked for a prolonged visit again, but my friends tell me that never happens two times in a row. *She is here!* I am asking the guard in service if I got the prolonged one. He nods, hooray!!!

My darling is beautiful as always.

"I miss you a lot!"

"I miss you too."

"How was the sailing?"

"It was fantastic! Pike is such a good skipper, we got along very well. He even took me snorkelling, can you believe?"

"I am so happy that you enjoyed the trip. Next time, let's go together. Probably not in Croatia though, I have enough of enjoying this otherwise lovely country."

"Ha, ha, yes, let's pick a different one, I agree." She smiles at me, and I feel that our connection keeps getting stronger. Weird, after a couple of weeks with bullet-proof glass between of us.

She moves to a different, more serious subject. "Honey, have you heard the news from Mr Zoran?"

"No, I haven't! What's on? He was here last week, said that the analysis will come soon but I haven't seen him since."

“It’s on the way! Apparently, the forensic analysis was completed and is being sent to the judge as we speak.” Jarka can’t hide her excitement, and obviously I cannot either.

My eyes get wet, as I am taken over by emotions. “If that’s true and the results are OK – it means that they will release us soon!”

I am hopeful but still try to manage my mind into *You will be still here for a couple of weeks* in order not to be disappointed later.

“What about you going back to Prague, huh? Now, after you successfully sailed around. I love to see you, obviously, but at the same time would feel relieved knowing that you are safe back home.”

“Listen, don’t annoy me,” she snaps back. “I am safe, nothing will happen to me. Except for meeting you, which obviously has happened already.”

A smile shows up on my face and she smiles too. “Don’t worry, Dan, I have to return anyway. My work is waiting, the company was super tolerant, but I feel it’s time to go back.”

“Oh, that’s right, of course. It’s so easy to forget here in the jail that ‘normal’ life goes on outside. Well, in that case, I hope to see you soon and be able to touch each other, finally.”

“Yes, I can’t wait too. Let’s touch multiple times and on multiple places…” she replies, and I feel that breaking the glass in front of me seems like a reasonable next step.

“What to say. I can’t wait too, my love. Let’s spend the rest of our lives together, shall we?” Nothing more cliché could come to me but I say it anyway.

She shakes her head and bids farewell: “I am not sure about the rest of our lives – as you know I am not able to plan anything – but let's definitely spend a lot of time in bed together after they let you go from here."

The sound of the baton hitting a metal chair interrupts our erotic conversation, and the 30 minutes are over.

"Love you."

"Love you too." Blowing a kiss into the air, she stands up, turns around, and walks out of the room. This was the last time that I saw her in the jail.

After the lunch there is a walk. I am curious to see what our provocateur will come up with. Our walk group consists of the three cells putting money together and ordering a football. We got it today! Kicking the ball around feels great, I love it. More importantly, my fitness is the best of all the guys, and I play reasonably well, which creates lots of respect in the group. Croatians are crazy about football! My 'enemy' runs a bit but then must stop, can't catch his breath. He has no time or energy to test me, which is good.

Every key rattle in the door makes me jump and think that I am going home. But not this time yet, it's lunch. After the meal, I am writing down and learning new Croatian words. I am sure that Ivo is doing the same. He likes languages too.

We can talk Croatian together after they release us, and nobody back home will understand. What a massive advantage gained after five weeks in jail!

Here is an overview of key words to master in case one ends up in the prison here:

- custody – pritvor
- investigation – istraga
- judge – sudac
- handcuffs – lisičine
- lawyer – odvjetnik

- defence by silence – braniti se šutnjom
- guard – komandir
- floor commander – komandir kata
- walk – šetnja
- cell – soba, celja
- shop – kantina
- penis – kurac
- butt – guzica
- visit – posjeta
- extended visit – produžena posjeta
- head of prison – upravitelj
- request – zamolja
- murder – ubojstvo
- I am not guilty – nisam kriv
- cell raid – prepad
- please – molim vas
- expertise – vještačenje
- fuck it – jebem to
- medic – liječnik
- prisoner – zatvorjenik
- accused – optuženik
- indictment – optužba
- drugs – droge
- to smoke – pušiti
- money – novac, lova, pare
- damned! – proklet!

Split, Zatvor Bilica, Dan's cell
16th of October 2002

Today started as usual with the wake-up call, a little stretching, a guard check of the cell, and breakfast. Nothing else to do…

When will this 'adventure' end?

I am hopeful that it will be soon. Nevertheless, one can't stop the mind coming up with all sorts of versions of what the future might look like.

We can stay here for 20 years. We can be released, and friends of the tragically deceased navy diver will kill us in revenge. I will slip in the shower… Stop it. Nothing else to be done beside wait.

I do a bit of exercise but I'm most definitely not in a positive mood today. At least my darling should be back in Prague by now!

Sleep a bit, read my book, watch TV, and wait for lunch. *I really don't know how people can survive many years in prison.* Of course, those who are guilty don't have the element of uncertainty, which is huge. Still, it's hard to imagine. *One must probably find some passion, something to keep them occupied both physically and mentally. Maybe meditation?* I am convinced that we people can manage anything, that we have to trust our abilities and intuition to help us out of any situation. It would be an interesting experience to learn how to survive decades of jail. An experience that is better to avoid though.

After lunch I fall asleep, only to be awoken by the clatter of the key in the door. The guard opens it and says with a faint smile on his face:

"Dan, gather your stuff. You are going home."

My brain is still foggy from an afternoon nap, but the words are clear. *I am going home!!!*

My mates are clapping, happy for me and at the same time obviously a bit envious that they must stay. With their crimes, they will probably not get out so fast.

A million things, a million thoughts are swirling in my mind. *Really? Is it really happening? I was looking forward to this moment, wishing for it to arrive as soon as possible. Now it's here and I am a little confused. I got completely used to the monotonous rhythm of prison life. After 'only' five weeks. How does one feel leaving prison after, say, 20 years? Frightening idea.*

"Goodbye, Dan, have fun out there and don't forget to run," says Dragan and hugs me.

"Enjoy the freedom, my friend," joins in Goran. "I will remember our discussion about universe and God forever. Thank you." He hugs me too.

"Goran, you are a good guy. I am happy that we met and hope that your case will get clear soon too. Good luck."

"Don't forget to organize an *izlaznica* when you are back home. With the roasted pig and beer and everything," comes from the last inmate, Vladimir. To my big surprise, he hugs me too.

Living five weeks together, every day, every minute in a small, intimate space of a prison cell creates a strange bond between men who had never met before.

One of the boys gets my shoelaces. He says that he will start running. Another gets my almost-full toothpaste and soap. The third one, who speaks English, gets some of my books.

I pack my stuff into a white sack from the guards. We say one last goodbye and I am out of the cell, standing in the corridor and looking back at their faces. We all know that we will most likely never see each other again.

I wonder how Ivo is doing and what it feels like for him to leave the cell. Obviously, I assume that we will see each other soon, that he is out too. What a story to tell our kids – if we ever have any!

Well, what to do next?

Let's go and truly appreciate freedom, for a change.

Epilogue

The seemingly terrible experience I am now grateful for – it made me think, it made me feel, it made me a better person. 'Dan before' is for sure very different to 'Dan after'. I hope it would not sound too arrogant, but it helped me to evolve from a person with (almost) no feelings into someone who truly feels and appreciates love, enjoys small things that bring happiness to life, and values the present moment.

Let's stay with the present moment for a bit. Past does not really exist for me, except for remembering beauty and happiness, moments of peace. I don't care about past too much. Future is something else – my mind is often occupied with future. There is work to be done here.

Another topic that stands out for me is survival. I was always interested in how people survive disasters, adverse conditions, being lost in nature, anything of that sort. There are many books on my shelf about survival skills and tactics. I have been reading and re-reading all of them and often asking myself *How would you react, Dan? How would you manage? Would you crack under pressure and give up or prevail, survive, and in a weird way even enjoy at least parts of the experience?* I have never lived through a true survival situation on my own. Until Croatia. It seems that I survived. My mind was the strongest weapon together with the ability to stay calm in almost any circumstances. Yes, I was getting emotional, sad, anxious, or distracted. Of course, I am human. Nevertheless, I have always been able to regain the peace of mind rather quickly and use breathing or meditation to get out of the hole. Luckily, my abilities and resolve did not get tested by a prolonged stay. Who knows how I would manage 20-plus years locked up for a crime that I did not commit?

Many events occurred in my life which most people would label as terrible, frightening, or awful, basically expressing some form of negative emotion. It has never ever occurred to me to use these labels. Why? What happens to us just happens. Very often we cannot influence it at all. Therefore, it does not make any sense to add labels, to feel pain or anger about something we did not influence, we did not cause. Everything that happens to us in our life is just an experience. We can decide how to process such experience, how to react, what to do next, what to learn (or not).

In this case, being in a jail falsely accused of murder was a profound experience.

An experience which brought a deeper understanding of myself and of how the world works and allowed me to experience love and beauty in intense ways that I have never felt before.

One more interesting reflection comes to mind – about the role of media in our societies. How important are media in revealing or clouding the truth. How difficult it might be for journalists to really do a good job and be non-judgemental about what they see around. How people trust what they read without critical thinking. How a suspected murder can be turned into 'this is what certainly happened' by one biased journalist and an editor who does not have a spine. How a war crimes tribunal can be so differently portrayed in various countries by media depending on where the popular opinion sits and whether or not journalists are emotionally attached to potential outcomes.

I am still very sad that two people died, but I am grateful that I was – in the process and for sure against my will or wish – given an opportunity to learn.

Jarka has done an amazing job of getting the right lawyer in place, helping my parents to deal with the situation, giving me much needed support and love. It meant a lot to me while I was behind bars. And yes, 'Foxy' and I got married and have two wonderful kids that I am truly proud of.

My parents and siblings were obviously shocked by what happened. They never believed that I would commit anything like what the media were talking about. They knew. I can only vaguely imagine how hard it was for them to face a situation of their innocent son and brother being in a Croatian jail and they couldn't help much. It could even have been emotionally worser for them than for me – after all, I was on a 'survival battlefield' fighting for my freedom while they had to sit at home and wait for the outcome.

My Unilever career developed very well for me after these events. Our chairwoman promoted me to lead the company's food division with a multi-million-euro turnover, and I assume it was not thanks to my stint in the prison. More importantly, my colleagues and friends were very supportive, helped Jarka with moral support, and raised money to cover her travel costs. I truly appreciate all the support and care.

Ivo and I stayed friends. We meet every year, have a beer (or two) together, discuss life and what matters, and from time to time memory lane takes us back to those days in Croatia. During the last time we saw each other in one of our favourite pubs in Prague city centre, the conversation swirled back to the jail time.

"Hey, do you remember that Croatian *pršut*, the one that we could buy at the prison shop in Split?" Ivo said while munching on Prague ham, which is not bad either, and accompanying it with a thorough sip of beer.

"Indeed, the ham was fantastic," I replied with my mouth full. "Those roasted shrimps that one could order from the restaurant too."

"Ha ha, I will never forget how I felt when one of the inmates in our room ordered food delivery into the jail. OMG, this can happen in Croatia only."

"Imagine we went sailing to Thailand and ended up in the jail there! All the great Thai food!" I teased him.

"Go to hell, buddy, I am never ever going to sail with you again." Ivo concluded our conversation which brought us right back to the Croatian life events.

Well… there was one more moment right after our arrival in Prague back in 2002, which is hard to describe with words. Let me try.

I printed and framed the picture of Michael. He was sitting in the sailboat cockpit on the day of his death. He was smiling to the afternoon sun and happily eating his portion of tuna. *It was the last image of him ever taken.*

One of the divers and I visited Michael's mum in her small, cozy apartment in Prague suburbs. She received the frame with shaking hands, and then we sat together in her living room.

I had nothing to say.

No words can capture what a mother feels when her child, her only child, is gone. Forever.

RIP, my friend.

THE END

Press release published by Dan and Ivo on 30th December 2002

The investigation of the death of a Czech diver is closed.

Two Czechs who were accused in September 2002 in Croatia of the murder of their diver friend Michael and spent five weeks in prison, received a statement from their lawyers in Croatia including an official confirmation from the Croatian public prosecutor's office closing the investigation of their case which was reached by the investigating judge in Split already in October. The analysis of the computer records and the results of the autopsy clearly showed that the death of the diver could not have occurred other than by suicide. According to the conclusions of the investigating judge, the murder was technically and timewise completely impossible. Other than that, there was no motive either, just speculation. The diver decided to commit suicide in a hopeless situation, after he lost his orientation in an underwater cave at a depth of about 40m and completely exhausted his supply of compressed air.

At the same time, both Czech citizens gave power of attorney to their legal representatives in Croatia to sue the newspaper *Slobodna Dalmacija*, which in the first days of their detention and investigation published their full names and printed articles in which the authors claimed that it was proven that they planned and committed the murder for reasons of homosexual jealousy, which was, of course, pure journalistic fantasy. The Croatian media covered the case even after the return of all detainees to the Czech Republic. *Slobodna Dalmacija*, for example, quoted one of the other crew members who complained about the incorrect procedure of the police. The chief of the Split police responded in a comprehensive open letter on 29/10/2002, in which he defended the police's actions and stated the initial indications that spoke against the two accused (a dead diver with a knife in his chest, a previously unrecorded manner of a diver's death – suicide, suspicious red spots on the boat and lie detector result) and at the same time added that there was no mention of homosexual motives by the police, he even called these articles manipulation and added that it would be interesting to know where the journalists got this information from. The analysis determined that the red stains were from the paint in the harbour, which was what all the other crew members had claimed from the beginning. Regarding the lie detector results, divers added that, in their opinion, the test was conducted in an incorrect manner, they had no idea that a violent death was being investigated, and the questions were purposely asked in a way to shock them.

It was only in the past few days that it was possible to pick up the diving equipment of all seven crew members. According to unconfirmed information, the investigation of the responsibility for the death of the Croatian diver-rescuer, who also perished in the cave, after he and his Croatian colleague went in search of the Czech diver, is still ongoing.

Acknowledgments

I've had this idea – to write a book about my experience – for more than 20 years. Thanks to friends who kept saying, "It's a book, it's a movie, write it down," and mainly thanks to Robin. I finally sat down in spring of 2023 to put the story on paper. Originally, it was supposed to be a couple of pages. Well, it became a book, and I am still in shock that it's here.

Thanks to all the dear people who read the text and gave me valuable input, namely Robin and Chris. Of course, massive thanks to James Andersen Banks, who had the patience to go through the editing process with me. Not easy! You can find his books on Amazon, and if you'd like to work with him as an editor, you can find him on Reedsy. The entire team at Rowanvale Books deserve all my gratitude - you made it happen.

I wrote the story to honour my diver friends who are no longer with us.

I will be forever grateful to Jarka, my wife and life companion. Her persistence and love saved me many times, not only in Croatia.

Thanks to my kids, who thoroughly edited the script and offered many valuable comments.

My scuba diving friends who were with me, you are stars. There were some difficult moments, but we stayed together and did everything possible to save our friend.

Ivo – Ivo, you remained a true friend, one of the best, despite me "inviting" you for the trip. Your thorough record of the events brought even more clarity to my forgetful mind.

My mom and dad, who watched and endured more than one hairy adventure situation that I put myself into.

Thank you.

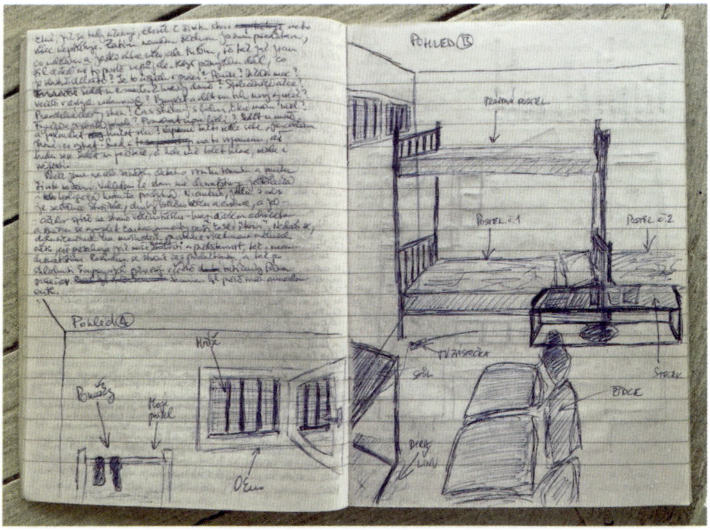

Prison cell drawings by Dan from September 2002

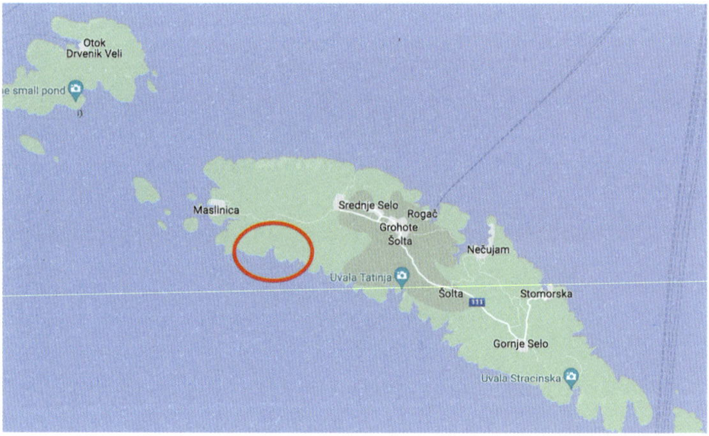

Island Solta, bay Poganica, Croatia (source: Google Maps)

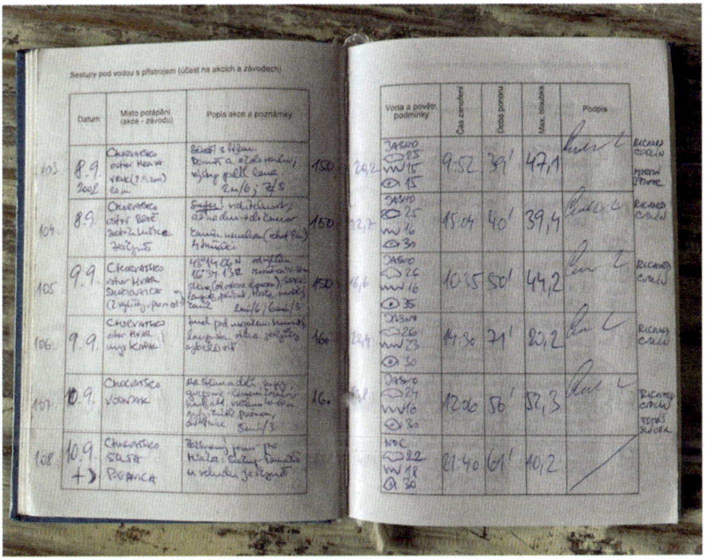

Dan's scuba journal with the 108th dive, an attempted search and rescue of Michael

An image from the airport of the author surrounded by media upon arrival in Prague, Czech Republic. (source: iDnes)

About Dan Frolec

The story depicted in this book is a tragic, yet true account of the events from 2002 that unfolded after Dan's friend got lost in an underwater cave in Croatia, and then, out of the blue, Dan and one of his other friends from the group became falsely suspected of murder and thrown into custody. Croatian police needed someone to blame. They claimed that they found the deceased friend with his diving knife in his chest. Dan's fight for freedom started.

Dan feels that hyperactivity is his superpower, enabling him to do a crazy number of things at the same time. He is a father of two brilliant kids and is aspiring to be a good husband. He loves sports, adventure, spending time with friends, reading, writing, being in the ocean, and (too) many other activities. He also continuously searches for peace of mind, with mixed results.

Life took Dan from his birthplace in Prague to many corners of the world. He has built a successful career in large, multinational companies. Then, in 2016, he quit the corporate world and moved to Bali with the whole family. The reason? Green School Bali for the kids — a truly special place with a unique approach to education. He started his own advisory firm and works with a small number of clients, helping them build better businesses. He also created an online fitness programme for better management of lower back pain called ExFitt.com.

He loves teaching freediving and riding motorcycles. Last, but definitely not least, three dogs and a cat are all part of the family.

You can find Dan on Instagram (@danfrolec) or on his website www.danfrolec.com.

What Did You Think of
The Cave: The True Story of Two Mysterious Deaths in an Underwater Labyrinth?

A big thank you for purchasing this book. I do hope you enjoyed it.

Book reviews are incredibly important for an author. All feedback helps us to improve our writing. Please spare a few minutes to post a review on Amazon and Goodreads. Your review would be much appreciated.

Publisher Information

rowanvale books

Rowanvale Books provides publishing services to independent authors, writers and poets all over the globe. We deliver a personal, honest and efficient service that allows authors to see their work published, while remaining in control of the process and retaining their creativity. By making publishing services available to authors in a cost-effective and ethical way, we at Rowanvale Books hope to ensure that the local, national and international community benefits from a steady stream of good quality literature.

For more information about us, our authors or our publications, please get in touch.

www.rowanvalebooks.com
info@rowanvalebooks.com